THE ART OF SPIRITUAL SNAKEHANDLING
and other sermons

James D. Glasse

ABINGDON
Nashville

THE ART OF SPIRITUAL SNAKEHANDLING

Copyright © 1978 by Abingdon

Library of Congress Cataloging in Publication Data

GLASSE, JAMES D
  The art of spiritual snakehandling, and other sermons.
    1. United Church of Christ—Sermons.   2. Sermons, English.   I.   Title.
  BX9886.Z6G562   252'.0834   78-12342

ISBN 0-687-01890-0.

Scripture quotations unless otherwise noted are from the Revised Standard Version of the Bible, copyrighted 1946, 1952, © 1971, 1973 by the Division of Christian Education of the National Council of the Churches of Christ in the U.S.A.

MANUFACTURED BY THE PARTHENON PRESS AT
NASHVILLE, TENNESSEE, UNITED STATES OF AMERICA

FOR

JAMES, JANET, JUDITH, JULIA
who grew up with my preaching
and helped me grow up as a preacher

CONTENTS

FOREWORD

Communication is at the very heart of the Christian experience. The Gospel of John states quite clearly that "In the beginning was the Word, . . . and the Word became flesh and dwelt among us." Phillips translated that statement: "At the beginning God expressed himself."

It's strange then that preaching seemed to fall into disfavor in many circles for the last few decades. We were told that this was a time for action, not words. As if you could ever really separate the word from the deed. Now once again the imperative in preaching has asserted itself in the theological certainty that the Word still becomes flesh and expresses itself.

Among those concerned with the quality and integrity of preaching is James Glasse. His sermons in this volume were preached at the Chautauqua Institution where preaching continues to be held in high regard. Dr. Glasse is president of a theological seminary, but first and foremost he is a pastor concerned with the whole Christian ministry.

For more than a century Chautauqua has been a forum where, in addition to the preaching services, there are also a variety of lectures by Jewish scholars and representatives of Eastern religions as well as

7

messages from a broad spectrum of political, educational, and cultural speakers. This microcosm of the world demands that the preacher speak with clarity and understanding as well as theological integrity. As the late Abraham Joshua Heschel said, "You cannot worship God with your body if you do not know how to worship him with your soul. The relationship between the deed and inner devotion must be understood in terms of polarity." This polarity implies that the deed becoming flesh is also known in and through the sermon.

The many thousands who assemble at Chautauqua come from a wide variety of cultural, theological, and sociological backgrounds. To speak to such listeners requires a skill that ought to be a significant emphasis in all preaching. At Chautauqua Dr. Glasse dramatized that skill. His sermon entitled "The Art of Spiritual Snakehandling" immediately spoke to the curiosity of these many persons. But then, with consummate skill, he poked through their interest and delight with his humor to the nub of the matter—their needs and concerns. If preaching falls into disrepute it is because some preachers dodge that nub; they think of the sermon as an amusing program filler instead of a sharing of the living Word with living persons.

In *The Ecology of Faith,* Joseph Sittler dedicated his lectures on preaching to his preacher-father, describing him in these words: "He lived with complete immediacy within the world of the Bible. He announced, administered, celebrated the Gospel in preaching. The biblical images required from him no demythologizing; he intuitively understood them as Godly powers. . . . They were living transcripts of how a gracious God dealt and deals with his erring and unfaithful children."

Dr. Glasse's sermons are examples of such living messages that deal with the human predicament with loving kindness and humor; and share again the glad good news of the possibility of experiencing the renewing and redeeming love of God.

Ralph W. Loew
Director, Department of Religion
Chautauqua Institution

PROLOGUE

A Nonintroduction

I have not tried to conceal the fact that this is a book of sermons. In fact, I have taken time in relation to a number of them to share some of the circumstances under which the particular sermon began and developed. But this is less a book of sermons and more a book about preaching.

If I were a local pastor, I might have more to say about the traditional discipline of preparing and delivering sermons, but for the past twenty-five years I have not been a pastor who preaches regularly to the same congregation. I have been a "traveling preacher," going from place to place, filling in for vacationing ministers, covering for ones who got sick, being invited to preach on special occasions like the anniversaries of congregations and the installations of pastors. I'm always just passing through.

Putting Preaching into Print

As a traveling preacher I have learned a number of things. It is a luxury of sorts to be able to preach the same sermon to a variety of congregations. Some of the sermons in this book have been in the making for over a decade. Several of them have been preached hundreds of times. Yet this is the first time I have ever tried to write a sermon. None of them were written for this book. They were prepared for the people to whom they were preached; therefore, what you find in this volume is as much the product of the people who have heard me preach as it is my own.

None of these sermons has really been written. They were first of all preached. Somebody had their tape recorder running, and the tapes were then transcribed and filed away. I think I had the thought in the back of my mind that sometime I would want to edit the transcriptions and put them together in a book. But it wasn't until the summer of 1977, when I was invited to be the visiting preacher at the Chautauqua Institution during a week in July, that a number of them came together at the same time. It is the custom at Chautauqua to tape and transcribe the sermons of visiting preachers. Thus, Ralph Loew and his staff presented me a rather substantial bundle of material. When I saw that much of it in mimeo, I was encouraged to look at some of the other transcriptions that I had filed away and, during Holy Week of 1978, I edited them into what is now this volume.

For a long time I didn't want to write down or publish my sermons because I was afraid I couldn't use them anymore. But now that they are about to go to press, I realize that I intend to keep preaching them. The fact that they are in print doesn't mean that they are dead anymore than preaching them a number of times in the past has seemed like a repetition.

As I look over the sermons I am aware that I never

prepared a sermon in general, but only in particular. That is, I never just sat down and wrote a sermon. Rather, some particular circumstance or instance called for comment, I responded to it by preaching in the context of worship, and something like a sermon resulted. In some of these instances I seemed to have stumbled on a seed that continues to grow. On other occasions I developed a sermon which I preached once, and never preached again. There are other sermons, like the one on spiritual snakehandling, which I have preached several hundred times under remarkably different auspices and occasions. I have put that one first, because it continues to be a growing thing for me, and the one for which I have had the most requests. Even now that it is in print, I do not consider it finished.

Can Preaching Save the Preacher?

In the Epilogue I will have more to say about preaching, with some professional observations on what I have learned in twenty-five years as a traveling preacher. But in this Prologue I want to reflect on some of the things preaching has done for me as a person. My public responsibility to proclam the gospel of Jesus Christ has been a way of fulfilling part of my private responsibility to hear and believe that same gospel. I see this happening in at least two ways.

First, having to preach has forced me to study, pray, and prepare myself for preaching. (There was a time when I thought I was preparing sermons. Now I know that I was really preparing myself.) And for a long time I put so much of myself into the task that I had no time or

13

energy left for myself. I was new at preaching and teaching. It took a lot of time and energy, and after I had finished preparing a sermon I was exhausted. But after delivering it, I was exhilarated. I take this to mean that preaching the gospel releases power. In giving it away a gift is received. This is very mysterious, but I have no doubt that preaching is what energized my life as a Christian minister and as a person.

But when I became a traveling preacher, I gave up preparing and delivering sermons. Relieved of the necessity of coming up with new material, I used the old sermons over and over and over. I began to hear the message more clearly myself when I had a chance to hear it again and again. I became aware that my public life as a preacher was doing things to my personal life as a Christian.

This second insight has been slow in coming. It still is not crystal clear to me. But here are, at least, some clues. As a traveling preacher I didn't have to worry about coming up with something new for the folks. An old standard, a golden oldie, spiced with some current and local reference, did just fine. I also had a chance to hear the message again. I began to learn things from my own preaching. Part of my message was for me!

In reading these sermons written down and in trying to edit them into readable prose, I have been surprised by how much of myself is in them. I appear to be my own best illustration! Does that sound like an ego trip? Certainly that is part of it. But there is more. Now I am becoming aware that I have been offering myself, not just my material, as an illustration of the power and work of God. I, myself, have been struggling for identity, purpose, hope, salvation. If salvation comes by preaching, then preachers ought to be saved by now. I have come to understand a little more how it is that salvation comes by the hearing of the Word. I most often hear the Word in my own voice, since I seldom hear anyone else preach! In this sense the voice of God has become my own voice. Preaching has taught me a lot about the gospel, and because of that I want every Christian to be a preacher, to find a way of working and witnessing that builds up the church—and saves our souls (II Timothy 4:11-16).

Finally, there is no theme to this book. At Chautauqua I was asked to declare a theme for the week. I told them to announce, "The Church, The Spirit, and Me." And I preached the six best sermons in my barrel. (For those who don't know what "sermon barrels" are, there's something about them in the Epilogue.) Later, when my publisher wanted a theme, I asked for the opportunity to offer a collection of sermons without a theme, and even to dramatize the differences among them. I have tried to show how each sermon is a unique response to an incident, event, occasion, or to a personal question or issue that disturbed or challenged me. I appreciate the generosity of my publisher in allowing me to publish the sermons without forcing them into a format. If there is a theme, it is a picture of myself wrestling with the scriptures, struggling with myself and then speaking as best I could out of that struggle. My first two books were about the ministry and for pastors. This one is about myself and for lay people. Many men and women who have heard me preach have asked for copies of what I have said. Here, finally, is something in print.

I offer this book as an act of devotion during Holy Week 1978 and as a gift to all those who have given me so much by supporting me with their prayers as I have tried to preach the gospel. But mostly, this collection is in gratitude to Lancaster Theological Seminary which has been the focus of my personal and professional life since 1970. Also, to the Chautauqua Institution whose invitation prompted the preaching of most of these sermons, and whose staff first taped and typed them. Finally, to Edna Hafer who has labored with me in the preparation of the manuscript. She, as much as anyone, has pressed me to get this book together. More than anyone, she has done the hard work of typing and editing which has made it a reality.

Easter Eve, 1978
Lancaster, Pennsylvania

I.

The Art of
Spiritual Snakehandling

(Jeremiah 9:23-24. I Corinthians 12:1-13, 27-31)

What kind of Christian are you? Have you ever thought
of yourself as an enthusiast, an egghead, a pray-er, or a
chicken-fryer? These are four kinds of "spiritual
snakehandlers" that I've observed in the church. The
purpose of this sermon is to help you understand
yourself as a spiritual snakehandler. But perhaps I
should begin with some familiar background questions
and issues.

One of the tasks of every Christian is to come to some
clarity about his or her place in the mission and
ministry of the church. As we say in the Statement of
Faith of the United Church of Christ: "God calls us into
his church, to accept the cost and joy of discipleship."
How are we to enter as disciples and servants into the
mission of the church?

The church has been given a broad commission to go
into all the world and preach the gospel to every
creature, but not one of us can go everywhere and to
everyone. The question is: What am *I* to do? This is a
question of personal identity. How I respond and *what* I
do turn critically on *who* I am? So how do I ever come to
that knowledge of myself which allows me to respond
and give myself fully and wholly to the work of God?

Paul, writing to the church of Rome, advised:

For by the grace given to me I bid every one among you not to think of himself more highly than he ought to think, but to think with sober judgment, each according to the measure of faith which God has assigned him. (Rom. 12:3)

When we seek that sober judgment, hypocrisy gets in the way. There are two kinds of hypocrisy. One is to pretend that I'm something that I'm not. This is properly called pretense. The other is to pretend that I'm *not* something that I am. We have misnamed this second form of hypocrisy "humility." It is not humility, but hypocrisy. Humility requires honesty. If I pretend that I am not something that I really am, then I am not honest. The point is not to put myself up or down, but to put myself forward in honesty. The point is that I be who I am, know who I am, and place myself at the disposal of God. This has always been a problem for me, but I now understand a little bit more about what I can do about it. I want to share with you three perspectives I have on this problem.

The first comes out of my present struggle as a middle-aged, middle-class, white, male, American, Protestant, Christian person in the identity crisis that besets me and my generation. The second I gained from watching some snakehandlers in a North Carolina church. The third came to me while reading Paul's first letter to his little church in Corinth. (Those of you who are programmed to listen to three point sermons will know that when I quit talking about myself and start talking about snakehandlers, we have moved from point one to point two. When I quit talking about snakehandlers and start talking about the apostle Paul, we have moved from point two to point three. And when we get there, you will know we are about through.)

I really thought that at my age I would have everything all worked out. I was led to believe that if I played out my life according to the script that had been written for me, when I got to middle-age I would really have it all together. So I did as I was told, got educated, ordained, married, employed. I got it all together. But now it won't stay together. Indeed, I am beginning to feel like my world is starting to fall apart. I'm finding out more things about myself now than I have known in my whole life before. Here are some of them.

I have discovered that I have a middle-class, middle-aged, white, male, American, Protestant, Christian *negative* self-identity. All my life I thought I knew who I was. But I didn't. I just knew who other people were, and by knowing I *wasn't* one of "them," I thought I knew who "we" were. That doesn't work for me anymore.

This is the way I used to think. First, I knew that I wasn't a Jew. That's how I was supposed to know that I was a Christian. So we told stories about Jews to make it clear who they were so that we would know we weren't like them. Next, I knew that I wasn't a Catholic. That's how I was supposed to know that I was a Protestant. So we told stories about them to make it clear who they were so we would know we weren't like that. Then I knew that I wasn't a Methodist, Episcopalian, or Baptist. That's how I was supposed to know that I was a Presbyterian. So we told stories about them to make it very clear we were not like them. I knew I was a boy because I wasn't a girl, and we told stories about them. I knew I was an American because

I wasn't a foreigner, and we told stories about them. I knew I was white, because I wasn't black, and we told stories about them.

We told stories about everybody. But we didn't tell stories about ourselves. Why should we? We were just people! But about everyone else in the world there was something special we had to know so we'd know who we were. This worked fine as long as they acted like they were supposed to; that is, my identity was secure as long as they played according to my script and acted out my stereotypes and my prejudices.

But they wouldn't always act like they were supposed to! I met Jews who didn't act like Jews were supposed to act, and all of a sudden I wasn't sure about Jews anymore. Then the Catholics wouldn't act like Catholics. They started eating meat on Friday and singing gospel songs. And the first time I met a Baptist who drank and an Episcopalian who didn't, it blew the whole thing. Then women wouldn't act like "ladies," and the blacks wouldn't act like "negroes." When *they* wouldn't act out *my* stereotypes, I didn't know who I was!

Suddenly I realized that I'd never given much attention to who I was. So now, I'm trying to discover what it is to "be myself." These are disciplines and arts that I never learned, so I have a whole new education before me. I expect to be wrestling with that one right on into the grave and never really have it wrapped up. It's exciting, and it's scary. It's growthful, and it's part of what I'm trying to find out.

The beginning for me was in attempting to come to an honest assessment of myself. I had learned so well that one of the ways you know you're somebody is that you're both different and better than somebody else. This suggests a way of putting "us" *up* by putting "them" *down*. That's what the Bible calls sin. Of course I'm against sin, but I'm also very much a part of it. That kind of sinning is a part of me. I want to learn to deal with my prejudices. I want to be saved from them.

I remember coming to a point in my life when I thought I had it made. I had arrived. I was born and raised in a Christian home. I had graduated from a fine church-related college and an Ivy League divinity school. I had been properly ordained by a mainline denomination and was sent, in the infinite administrative wisdom of the Home Mission Board, to a little rural parish in North Carolina where I ran into people like I had never met before. I was ready for Jews, Catholics, etc. But here were people like me who were white and Protestant. They *looked* like us, but they didn't *act* like us. They did all sorts of things I'd never seen before. They spoke in tongues. They handled snakes. They healed each other. They saved souls. They had fried chicken suppers. They had revivals. They did all sorts of odd things I'd never heard of. I was raised up North among Presbyterians (God's frozen people). "We" didn't do things like that. So here I was, down South, among these warm and wonderful folk. I knew exactly what I had to do. I had to find out who "they" were so I would know who "I" was. (Here we go to point two of the sermon.)

The snakehandlers fascinated me most of all. "Oh these poor, primitive, superstitious people," I thought, "I have come down here to liberate them." The first thing I discovered was that they thought they had a better religion than mine. The second thing I discovered was that they didn't call themselves snakehandlers. They just called themselves Christians. My fascination with them led me to get to know them as persons in the community. They were really very nice people, by and large, and I saw that a whole lot other than their snakehandling was important to them. But when they went into the church building and did their special thing they acted out a particular form of sin. They had found one verse in the Bible that taught them how to tell who was a real believer and who wasn't. If you could take the snakes out of the box and handle them and put them back—you were in. If you didn't have enough faith to try, you hadn't made it yet. And if you did try and got bit—sorry about that. You may not like it, but the answer is clear. Yes, we laugh at them, "Those poor, primitive people," we say. But are *they* really much different from *us* ?

As I looked closely at what they were doing I came to see that everybody I had known in the Christian church up to that time was a snakehandler at heart. The difference is that they use *real* snakes, and we use what I call *spiritual* snakes. We practice the art of spiritual snakehandling. We have other things you have to "handle" in order to be a first-class Christian. This opened up a whole new way of looking at sin in the church. And there's so much of it in the church that we don't have to go outside to find it. There is no pride like spiritual pride, and there are really no snakes like spiritual snakes. Armed with this insight, I began seeing snakehandlers everywhere—even in the Bible. While reading I Corinthians it suddenly dawned on me that Paul had dealt with this same problem of spiritual snakehandling. In the thirteenth chapter of I Corinthians, I saw four groups of spiritual snakehandlers, which I call the enthusiasts, the eggheads, the pray-ers, and the chicken fryers—four different ways in which spiritual pride, spiritual snakehandling, was working in the church at Corinth. (You three-point sermon people have noticed that we are now at point three.)

Imagine, if you will, the congregation at Corinth. Each of the four groups is gathered in its own corner of the room. Each is doing its own thing.

First let's hear from the enthusiasts (the tongue-speakers?). They say, "Yes, we are all Christians here. We all believe in Jesus, we read the Bible, and we are trying to do the best we can. But you and I know that *enthusiasm* is the most important thing in the Christian life. Those of us who are really full of the spirit know that. Sometimes when we're talking about our faith we get carried away and start talking in languages you don't even understand. Now it's the people who have *that* kind of faith who are the first-class Christians around here."

Back in the other corner there's a quiet group of eggheads (Presbyterian types?). They look up from their books for a moment, and say: "That's very interesting the way you are acting over there. We also believe that there is a place for emotion in religion. We are not at all sure what that place is, but isn't it really more important that we understand our faith? Its biblical basis, its theological shape, its historical development, and its contemporary ethical relevance? Isn't it more important that we be able to make on behalf of the faith, not scrambled, babbling statements

23

of enthusiasm, but clear, cogent, and responsible statements. Now it's those of us who have this kind of *understanding* that really are the first-class Christians."

Over in the back there's a group down on their knees, praying. They look up just long enough to look down their noses, and say, "Yes, enthusiasm is fine, and all those theological ideas are interesting, but you and I know that it's *prayer* that matters. When the church moves forward, it moves forward on its knees. It is those of us who have mastered the art of prayer who are onto the real thing. When we pray, people get well. God hears us and answers us. Where would the church be without the spiritual empowerment of our kind of praying? We are the ones who really understand what it's about. We are the first-class Christians."

Then over in the corner, by the door near the kitchen, there are some people that are looking down their noses at everybody. They say: "All that enthusiasm is fine, and all that theology is interesting. We get worked up once in awhile, and we read the lessons. Every once in awhile we even know what the preacher is talking about. We pray morning and evening. We haven't moved any mountains lately, but you and I know that when there's some *work* to be done down at the church, something real, something important—like cooking a meal, or painting a wall, or mowing the grass—things that really matter in the church—we are the ones who are there. We are the ones who understand what is really important. We are the first-class Christians."

Look what Paul wrote to a church where the people were talking to each other like that:

If I speak in the tongues of men and of angels [the enthusiasts], but have not love, I am a noisy gong or a clanging cymbal. And if I have prophetic powers, and understand all mysteries and all knowledge [there are your eggheads], and if I have all faith, so as to remove mountains [pray-ers], but have not love, I am nothing. If I give away all I have, and if I deliver my body to be burned [that's where the chicken frying comes in], but have not love, I gain nothing. (I Cor. 13:1-3)

Now what was happening? Paul had come to Corinth and preached the gospel. Nobody had ever heard it before. It was a brand new thing. Some of those who heard it believed it, and some of those who believed it joined up, forming a community called a church. They didn't exactly know what that meant because, individually, each one had grasped for the gospel with what they had to grab with. The gospel struck something in them that made them know who they were and that gave them a new sense of themselves. Some were attracted by the spirituality and entered into that. Others were turned on to the ideas and focused on them. Others were drawn by the possibilities of prayer. Still others by the need for community survival and gave what gifts they had. What a beautiful thing!

Yet when all these sorts and conditions of men and women and children came together, they started fighting! Why? Because each was so intimately aware of how he or she had come into it and what that meant to them. Long before Dial soap they had started to think like the commercial: "You use Dial. Don't you wish everybody did?" I speak in tongues. Why doesn't everybody? Theology turns me on. What's the matter with you? I pray a lot. Why weren't you at prayer meeting? We were working down at the church. Where were you? So the very gifts they were given became the basis of conflict within the church. Now what are we to do?

Paul could have said, "In the interest of getting along together let's all deny our gifts. Let's just act like we all see the same thing, and feel the same thing, and care about the same things, and know the same things. Let's find the lowest common denominator of our experience, get together on that, and just not talk about those things that divide us." Thank God he didn't say that! What he said was, "I will show you a more excellent way." Bring your gift. Celebrate your gift, but go beyond it. Each individual gift marks us differently, and each of us is different from every one else. No two of us are the same. But while each of us is given a gift that makes us different, so everyone is given a common gift. Paul called that gift love. We know that. We wouldn't have fighting in the church if we always loved each other. There's no point in telling people that they ought to love each other, we already know this. But the problem is that we don't always love each other. What are we going to do about that?

First of all it involves loving myself and accepting myself. I am a creation of God, unique and precious in God's sight and therefore worthy of my own acceptance. I also know that every other creature of God bears that same mark—unique, peculiar, special, and valued by God. Love is the recognition of that. But what is love? I want to refer to one of the things Paul says about love: "Love is patient and kind; love is not jealous or boastful; it is not arrogant or rude. *Love does not insist on its own way* " (I Cor. 13:4-5). In our life together in the church, and in our life together as Christians in the world, we can be ourselves and do it our way, and yet not insist that everybody else do it our way.

Further along Paul gives us another clue. He has quit giving advice, he is simply giving a word of testimony. "For I am the least of the apostles, unfit to be called an apostle, because I persecuted the church of God. But by the grace of God I am what I am, and his grace toward me was not in vain" (I Cor. 15:9-10). That doesn't sound like very much. These are words that never would have moved me when I was younger, but they move me now. There was a time when I wanted my life to count. I wanted the world to be different and better because of my having lived. I wanted to take my gift and do something smashing with it. Now, with Paul, I just want to make sure I don't waste it. I want some assurance that it hasn't been given to me in vain, that it hasn't been lost. I've discovered that the main way I lose and waste my gift is in trying to assert it as the way somebody else ought to live and act: to spend all my energy trying to convince other people that they ought to see what I see, feel what I feel, know what I know, and do what I do.

I've also discovered that the best way I can use and multiply my gift is to use it as best I can, and not try to get anybody else to be just like me; but instead appreciate who they are and count on them to be just that—no more, no less. There's a choir up there in the choir loft who can sing, so we don't have to do that. Isn't that neat? There's somebody down in the basement taking care of the kids right now. That's great, because we don't have to do that. Out back there is someone teaching Sunday school, so we aren't doing that. That's what makes the church so rich and confusing—and frustrating. Something in me wants it simple, and yet something in me wants it rich.

There's a spiritual snakehandler in me—sometimes its an enthusiasm, sometimes it's an idea, sometimes it's a prayer, or sometimes it's a job I want to do. The snakehandler in me wants everybody else to agree with me, follow me, and do what I want to do. But there's also a loving Christian in me that wants all the variety of gifts to be expressed. And I say with Paul, "By the grace of God, I am what I am." And I say to you, "By the grace of God you are what you are." And I pray for you and me that his gifts to us will not have been given in vain.

Servants of the Spirit

Winds of Doctrine and Whirlwinds of the Spirit

(I Kings 19:9-12. John 3:5-12)

I want to speak of the Spirit, but I do not know exactly how to do that. By disposition I am not a mystical person, and yet I deal with the Spirit. I am not given to visions and dreams, and yet I know something of the power and presence of the Spirit. How can I speak of the Spirit in a meaningful way?

In trying to help Nicodemus understand something of the Spirit, Jesus asked him: "If I have told you earthly things and you do not believe, how can you believe if I tell you heavenly things?" (John 3:12). I will share with you an "earthly thing" that I learned from watching windmills. It's an image that helps me understand myself, the people in my life, and some ways the Spirit is moving among us. I hope it will help you, too.

The image took shape on the back seat of a bus in Holland in September 1973—a rather unlikely place for a spiritual insight to begin. One of the features of our curriculum at Lancaster Theological Seminary is a Seminar Abroad. For more than a decade we have required the senior class to spend the first month of their last year overseas with a faculty member. In 1973 it was my turn to take a group of twenty-five seminarians to Holland. One of them was a young man named Brad Lutz. He and I had fallen into several conversations about ministry and faith, theology and prayer. As we rode back to our hostel after spending all day looking at windmills, we talked about what we had seen and heard. At almost the same moment it came to both of us that in those windmills was a clue to some things we were trying to understand and express. The ideas that began in this conversation have been like seeds planted in rich soil. They continue to grow and bear fruit. I would like to share these insights with you now.

Brad and I had become aware that in Holland there is little hydroelectric power and only limited sources of fossil fuels. So, in times past, a major source of energy was the wind. Some of the Dutch put up their sails to catch the winds and were carried across the sea to find and found an empire. Others stayed at home and built windmills to harness the wind that blows from the North Sea. Using the power of the wind, they built their country. It dawned on us that in the scriptures, in both the Old and New Testament, the Hebrew and Greek words wind and spirit are the same. This is how the seed was planted. We began to imagine how to express a sense of the Spirit in the language of wind. We saw four things in the windmills that expressed our understanding of the Spirit and ourselves.

The first thing that struck us about windmills is their solid construction. They are rooted in the ground on solid foundations, built with very heavy timbers, and set down in a particular place. They are built so that when the wind blows they will not move or blow over. Locked into a particular piece of ground, they are designed to stay put.

The second thing is that even though the windmill can't go anywhere, it has the ability to turn its top all the way around—360 degrees. It can't change its location but it can change its orientation, and it can catch winds from any direction.

Thirdly, windmills have great arms or fans that are light and strong reaching out to the wind. The mill operator can run out more sail to catch even the lightest wisp of wind on a calm day, but equally important is the ability to pull in the sails when the gales hit and the wind becomes fierce, the ability to simply hold steady in the storm. In most windmills there is a braking device to stop the movement of the mill lest a hard wind turn the mechanism so fast that it is destroyed.

Fourthly, of the windmills we saw, each one was made for a specific purpose. If they wanted to pump water and grind grain in one place, they built two windmills, one to pump water and another to grind grain.

These four things set me thinking about how it is that we, who are rooted in the earth with real limits on our ability to move and change and grow, can attune our lives to catch the winds of the Spirit as they blow. So think with me now about these four things and how they relate to your life and mine.

First, that business about being heavily built and set down in one place. I've always been heavily built. But I've never really stayed in one place. As a member of a nuclear family, I hit the ground running. We never really came to rest anywhere, never belonged anywhere, never really put our feet down, never really unpacked! Now, partly as a function of my age and partly as a function of my vocation, I have a feeling that I am where I need to be. The time has come for me to put down roots—to see one particular place as the setting for my mission and my ministry. I'm trying to understand what it means to settle into one place. Like the windmill I can't keep running around to catch the wind, I must learn to wait patiently, where I am, for whatever winds of the Spirit come my way. God's spirit comes to me where I am to empower me here and now for what I am to be and do.

Secondly, although we are set down in a particular place, like the windmill we can turn ourselves all the way around to catch wind from whichever direction it blows. I am learning that once I put down my roots, I am open to a whole lot of new things. For instance, I can learn a lot from people I never took seriously. Women! What do they know? I'm learning a lot from the women in my life. And children! What do they know? As a grandfather I now see how much I always learned from my children, but could never admit. And Catholics! What do they know? We didn't even play with them when we were kids. Now I pray with them, they are not "them" anymore—but "us" in faith and fellowship. And Jews, and businessmen, and lay people. What do they know?

I never saw myself as terribly rigid or prejudiced, and I *was* pretty liberal in many ways, but I had a stiff neck and blinders. There were directions in which I never looked. Now I'm free to turn in all directions, to taste the fresh breeze of many "winds of doctrine"—and sense the Spirit in them.

For me, these two parts of the windmill go together. It appears that only as I am clearly rooted and grounded, do I have a basis from which to appreciate a wide variety of perspectives and points of view. So now when I look at myself and the world around me, and at what God seems to be doing among us in so many different ways, I try to take very seriously who I am, where I am, and where my feet are put down. But I also try to look and to listen—to be open to influences and points of view that once seemed either strange or foreign or false. Curiously enough, I think that in my latter years I am becoming more open and less defensive, more able to listen to a variety of points of view. And I take this to be a gift of the Spirit.

Thirdly, there is the ability to put out sail and catch the wind when it's slight, and the ability to pull in the sail and put on the brakes when it's too strong. I've seen windmills in Holland, just standing there—no wind. That's a picture of how I often feel, just hanging there—no Spirit. Just as I know a windmill can't turn itself, but must wait for the wind, so I know I have to learn to wait for the Spirit. I want to learn what it means to be still and see myself as a servant of the Spirit. I am learning that I do have some sail I can put out. I'm learning more about prayer and the ways in which I am supported by the prayers of others. I am now aware that there has been a lot of Spirit blowing in my life of which I have been unaware. I am also learning that God doesn't want me destroyed physically, spiritually, or intellectually. Like the windmill that has a device for slowing down and stopping when the wind gets too heavy, I have learned there are ways I can pull in, hang on, and let the storm blow over.

I was preaching not long ago in one of our United Church of Christ congregations in Pennsylvania. They were following the traditional Reformed service for Sunday, when suddenly a bunch of little kids in pink choir robes jumped up and ran to the front of the church. Accompanied by a piano, they began to sing a jazzy gospel hymn. It was something like, "When we meet Jesus at the corner of Gospel Avenue and Hallelujah Street." I thought it was really dreadful. I could see some of the folks out there in the congregation pulling in their sails and putting on the brakes! And, as if that wasn't bad enough, the leader brightly announced that they were going to teach us all to sing the song. The little kids ran out into the aisles and took their places at the ends of the pews. As they tried to get the old folks into the spirit of the thing, I could just see the agenda for the consistory meeting taking shape right there—"Whoever let those kids . . . !"

We people in the church have a real ability to pull in our sails, put on our brakes, and hang on. I've discovered that it is a very important spiritual discipline to take only as much as I can handle, and maybe just a bit more. I am prepared to strain and stretch a little, but I'm not going to take on any more than I can handle at one time. It's comforting for me to know that I have those disciplines and defenses. They are psychological devices which I have been carefully learning all my life. They are also God-given disciplines for spiritual growth.

When there is more than I can handle I pull in my sails and put on the brakes and the wind still blows. But most days the wind is neither gusting nor becalming. The wind blows, God's Spirit moves, God's presence and power come in ways which I have come to know, believe, and expect. They come to me through the quiet reading of the Bible and through what praying I do. They come in relationships with persons and in the life of the Christian community. They come to me in all kinds of ways which I sometimes overlook because they do not seem special or exciting. But now it is also important for me to understand that I can make adjustments in my life in relation to the Spirit just as the windmill can adjust itself to the wind. I am learning better how to put up more sail, how to reach out more, how to catch some winds I didn't feel before. I am also learning how to hold myself together, to feel some new strengths in myself.

Fourthly, and this brings us back to earth again, each windmill is set down in a particular place to perform a particular function. I find that as I continue to grow in grace, to increase in my understanding of the Christian life, to be more aware of the presence of God's Spirit in my own life, I am also finding specific confirmation of my own vocation and my own gifts. I have a sense that I am where God wants me to be and when I am there, seeking to do what I have been set down to do, then I'm given the power to do it. There are times when I wish I was some other windmill in some other place. But more and more I am coming to treasure myself and to rejoice in the way in which God has made others. It's like looking down the canal and seeing another windmill turning. I'm not the only one pumping water. I look across the field and see another windmill. I'm not the only one grinding grain. And that windmill way over there, I don't even know what it's doing. But it is turning. The Spirit is moving us all, and maybe some day I'll know *what* wind is blowing. It is as mysterious now as when Jesus said to Nicodemus: "The wind blows where it wills, and you hear the sound of it, but you do not know whence it comes or whither it goes; so it is with . . . the Spirit" (John 3:8). I consider the windmill. Without the wind it is a lifeless machine sitting idly in the field. It has potential, but no power. Then the wind comes with power. It does not change the nature of the windmill, nor move it to another location, but empowers it for useful work. And so I consider myself. Without the Spirit I am all potential and no power. I wait for the Spirit. The Spirit moves. It does not change my nature, nor bid me move to a new location. I am affirmed as I am, where I am, and empowered for the work of the Kingdom.

I do not always know from whence it comes or where it goes, but I am certain that as I wait for the Spirit as the windmill waits for the wind, as I make myself a servant of the Spirit, I shall be empowered to do what God has for me to do with my life. And for now that is enough.

"Can We Learn to Fight Like Christians in the Church?"

The focus of this meditation is conflict and controversy in the church. As a point of departure I'll begin with two scripture passages.

First from Jeremiah:

They have healed the wound of my people lightly, saying, "Peace, peace," when there is no peace. (8:11)

Then from Matthew:

Do not think that I have come to bring peace on earth; I have not come to bring peace, but a sword. For I have come to set a man against his father, and a daughter against her mother, and a daughter-in-law against her mother-in-law; and a man's foes will be those of his own household. He who loves father or mother more than me is not worthy of me; and he who does not take his cross and follow me is not worthy of me. He who finds his life will lose it, and he who loses his life for my sake will find it. (10:34-39)

Using these two scriptures I'll focus on the following questions: (1) What is the fight about? (2) What does it mean to fight in the church? (3) What does it mean to fight like Christians in the Church? All of these come together in the critical question: Can we learn to fight like Christians in the Church?

37

First, let me make it clear that I consider the present conflict and controversy in the mainline Protestant denominations to be a healthy condition and not a problem to be solved. Conflict is a sign of life, a symptom of a deeper vitality. If we can move toward our conflicts and touch them, we will be empowered for our tasks in the mission of the church. (I don't expect you to believe me just because I say so, but I hope you will listen to what I have to say.)

Secondly, I want to make it clear that I believe the answer to the question I am raising in this sermon is *yes.* Although we have learned to avoid fighting in the church, I am convinced that we can learn to fight in ways that build up the body of Christ for mission and ministry. (Once again, I do not expect you to agree with what I say, but I hope you will try to understand what I mean.)

Now—*What is the fight about?* Where does conflict and controversy come from? First of all, I believe it comes from the way in which God has made us. I believe, as it says in the book of Genesis, that we are made in the image of God, not in the image of each other. Each of us is a unique and a peculiar creation. No two of us are alike. That means no two of us ever see things the same or feel things the same or know things the same or believe things the same. No matter how much sameness we impose by dress, language, custom, etc., we remain unique persons, we are always something of a mystery to ourselves and others.

There is a song in a popular musical comedy that says people "can stand nose to nose for days and days and never see eye to eye." Some people believe that the longer we know each other the more similar we become in our looks, attitudes, and ideas. But I doubt that because, even if we "put our heads together," with your head right next to mine, there's still just enough difference in our angle of vision that we see things differently. This is true physically, intellectually, and spiritually. We are made differently by God. And that God-given difference lies at the heart of human conflict and controversy. The difference is good, but when we are tempted to corrupt the good with pride, that is sin. Sin suggests that my point of view is not peculiar, but is simply "the way things really are." Have you ever been in a conversation where people are saying how they feel about things, and everyone is sharing experiences? It's going very nicely when a seemingly peaceful, parental Christian says, "Now, we have heard your point of view, and your point of view, and this is all wonderful, but now, let me tell you how it is." Much of the conflict and controversy in the church comes from people who (often unconsciously) are trying to deny the differences among us and therefore deny part of the beauty of God's creation in each of us.

Secondly, some of the conflict in the church comes out of new things that are happening to us—things that we do not yet understand and which we cannot yet handle. I do not believe that we are suffering from a failure of national character or a decline of morals, but we are experiencing a lot of friction that comes from the freedom we have. We are running into more different kinds of people than ever before. It used to be possible to live in a closed, quiet, little world. Our world was just "us." All of "them" were out there somewhere, and we never had to deal with them. Now we look at TV, and "they" are in *our* living room. We open a magazine and there they are, in color and black and white. Now the family company doesn't just keep us in Rochester for life, but ships us off to places like Kingsport, Tennessee and Lancaster, Pennsylvania and Keokuk, Iowa and God knows where. We meet kinds of people we have never met before. What we are experiencing is not a failure of character, but a function of life style. As the pace and variety of movement increases there are more people running around and rubbing into each other. There is a whole lot more friction and conflict. It's not that people are meaner or more hateful, it's just that we are into so many new things that we don't understand and can't handle.

Thirdly, some of the fighting is rooted in residues of old antagonisms. Buried deep within us are suspicions and fears about "them"—who they are and what they are up to—nation against nation, race against race, religion against religion. These ancient tensions do not go away when we try to repress them. When we move away from them we have not moved beyond them. We carry the roots of prejudice and the fruit of fear deep within us. Though they may not control us, still they affect us.

Finally, as if all this isn't enough, there is the Christian faith. The text from Matthew makes clear that when the call comes to us to commit ourselves wholly to Christ, every other commitment and loyalty is then in conflict with our new one. The gospel challenges the natural and habitual ways we relate to each other in families, nations, churches, etc. The gospel is not preached to create trouble. It is not designed to destroy all traditional relationships. But it does disturb them. So the church, which comes in the name of the Prince of Peace, disturbs a lot of folks by calling for new commitments. The Christian gospel itself, and the seriousness with which we take it, is part of the trouble. What are we to do? Are we to act as if we were not created differently? Are we to pretend that we are not disturbed and confused? Are we to deny that we still hold on to ancient hatreds and fears and suspicions? Are we to act as though the gospel had not placed us in conflict with many things both inside and outside the church?

We fight not because we have become cantankerous, mean, and hateful, but because we are into so much change, with so many different kinds of people and in so many different ways, that it feels like fighting. And it feels that way because it is a fight! I do not think conflict will go away. In fact, I think it will get worse before it gets better, and I believe there will be more division. So the question is: Can we learn to live in this kind of tension and conflict? Can we learn to fight like Christians in the church?

Some of us have been told all our lives: "You shouldn't talk that way in the church. It will get people all worked up and disturbed. It might even split the congregation." I was raised that way, and something in me wants to believe that. But I'm also aware that when I express my anger in church, people don't look very worked up and disturbed to me. Most church people I know can handle a lot of conflict—even in church on Sunday morning. There is stability in the church we can count on. Never forget that.

Despite all the ways in which we seem to be changing, there's something deep inside us that just doesn't change. It holds us together way down inside, when up in our heads we think we are coming apart. This is one of the remarkable realities I experience in the United Church of Christ. We have wonderful roots and pillars from the German Reformed tradition, the Pilgrim Congregational experience, the Evangelical Synod, and the Christian churches. Up front and on top we have an official denominational identity crisis. We act like we don't know who we are. But the reason we are able to hang in there and play that kind of game on the surface is because we have our feet on something solid way down where our roots are.

A second major question is: *How do we do this in the church?* Some people say, "We shouldn't fight in church. The world out there is full of trouble and strain and controversy. And we want to come into the church and close the door to get away from all that." I'd like to do that too, and every once in a while I can pull it off. Once in a while we come into church and close the door. We turn on the organ music ever so quietly, let the stained glass colors wash over us, and the preacher's voice carries us into a peaceful reverie. But I also know that nothing miraculous happens to me just because I have walked through that church door. When I come in I bring the world with me. I bring my hopes, my fears, my anxieties, and my dreams. So does everybody else. Praise God that there are moments of peace and calm when the Lord is present in power to calm the storm. Do you remember the text, "They discovered in that moment of peace that they didn't have enough faith to sustain them in the storm." My prayer for the church in our time is that we have enough faith to live in the storm. How can we carry out a ministry of reconciliation if we shrink from strife? A first step is to reckon with how much conflict we can learn to tolerate. Next we can learn to use conflict skillfully in ministry.

I have been in the church all my life. I grew up in the church and lived in a parsonage. I'm a product of the church. I came right up through the chairs. I don't know much about what's going on out in the world, but I do know that in the church Christians fight about almost anything. They fight about whether to get a new hymnal or not, about the color of the rug, and about whether to sing a hymn to one tune or another. I have always seen a lot of conflict in the church. And I've observed that people who claim they can't handle conflict in the church can handle it in other parts of their lives. I am simply suggesting that we take what we have learned in the world and apply it in the church. Then maybe we can apply in the world what we have learned in the church.

American society is really a very conflicted society. It is designed that way. Our system of government is not centered in a monarchy, but is delicately balanced between three kinds of power that are always in tension and conflict with each other. Our economic system is not planned for stability but for competition. And many Americans have come to believe that good things come when people fight for their market, but that bad things happen when the system is planned, that conflict produces not only lots of goods but the good life. Sports are also a form of conflict. Courts of law are based on the assumption that justice comes out of the conflict between prosecution and defense.

We have designed these several ways to domesticate

conflict and controversy for fun and for profit. And I ask myself: Can we learn to do this in the church? Can we find a way to wrestle with each other about what we believe in so that we produce not simply baseball games or more money for the economy or even justice for society, but something like the kingdom of God and the fruits of the Spirit?

Watching my new grandson has reminded me how tremendously difficult it was to learn all the things I now take for granted: how to put food in my mouth and not in my ear, how to walk and talk. Everything we do now we learned as children. We've been carefully taught. We've learned our lessons well: how to avoid, how to deny, how to repress, how to displace, all these things. Can we learn a different way now? I think we can.

I've discovered that we can enter into almost anything if we think it's a game, if we know that we can start and stop it, if we know that somebody's in charge, and if we believe people will play fair according to the rules. In such a safe context people are much more ready to enter into new behaviors. So I've invented a simple game with four principles: consideration, containment, clarity, and commitment. By playing it we can learn to fight like Christians in the church.

The first principle is *consideration*. Paul says, "When you come together it is not for the better but for the worse. For, in the first place, when you assemble as a church, I hear that there are divisions among you; and I partly believe it for there must be factions among you in order that those who are genuine among you may be recognized. When you meet together, it is not the Lord's Supper you eat. For in eating, each one goes ahead with his own meal, and one is hungry and the other is drunk. . . . *Wait for one another* " (I Corinthians 11:17-21, 33, *my emphasis*). That's consideration.

We need rules for church meetings to protect groups against people like me—the fighters—those highly verbal, highly hostile types who jump in and take over. There has to be a way to make sure that everyone is given a chance to participate. So we need some rules. The two rules I suggest are called "rounds" and "tickets." Here's how they work. Conflict develops in the form of an argument. Three or four of the fast draw experts (the lawyers, the salesmen, the teachers, the preachers—the people who make their money with their mouths) have taken over the meeting. But those who are really much deeper and more careful thinkers, those who really understand things better but can't say them quite so quickly, are sitting there getting quieter and quieter, and madder and madder. At that point whoever is in charge has to spell out the rules for rounds. The leader can say, "All right, we've heard from all the verbal ones. Now, is there anyone else who has something to say in this round before we let the talkers say something again?" The notion here is that everyone has a right to say something, but nobody has a right to speak again until everybody has had a chance. (Rounds also protect the group from quiet people, those who just sit there and annoy the group with their silence.)

Another device is to give people tickets. If you decide you're going to fight for thirty minutes and you have ten people in the group, then everybody has three minutes to speak. So each person is given three tickets worth a minute apiece. And you have a timekeeper. (That's another way of involving people in a fight: give them a

45

role to play which allows them to watch and to hang in with the group without getting too involved.) How does this actually work? Well, there are some who want to get the discussion started right, so they use all their tickets at the start. There are the political types who sneak them in one at a time at strategic moments. Then there are those who hold all their tickets until the end to make sure that they have the last word. I've been in groups where some who have learned a lot about fighting like Christians actually gave their tickets to somebody else! Tickets and rounds are two ways that help make sure the group practices the principle of consideration because they insure that all persons in the group have an opportunity to participate.

The second principle is *containment.* One reason why a lot of people don't want to get into any kind of fight in the church is that they've been in church fights before that got out of hand. You don't want to start a fight because you don't know how to stop it. Hear this text. It is one of my favorites. "God is faithful, and he will not let you be tempted beyond your strength, but with the temptation will also provide the way of escape" (I Cor. 10:13). This means that it's unchristian for us to get persons into anything they can't get out of. I believe that anything is tolerable if the end is in sight. There has to be a contract about containment that makes clear when the fight begins and ends. Even if you don't like it, you can at least hang on and look at your watch until it's over. Timekeepers help the group to play fair according to the rules.

The third principle is *clarity.* I am convinced that much of the conflict in the church emerges because people try to agree too quickly. When we rush to agree too quickly, we relate at superficial levels which can't sustain relationships under stress. Premature agreement is just as conflicting as premature disagreement. So care must be taken to ensure clarity in communication. The simplest device I know is to make it a rule that no one has the right to agree or disagree with another person until they've been able to state that other person's position to his or her satisfaction. That's hard. Indeed, it is. But unless we're prepared to care that much about understanding each other, we're not prepared to learn to fight like Christians in the church.

A characteristic of Christian conflict is that understanding is much more important than agreement. The goal is not for me to agree with you, but for me to understand you. Personally, I would rather be disagreed with by someone who understands me than be agreed with by someone who doesn't. It's the depth of our caring that drives us to deeper levels of life in the church to the place where God wants us to be. Conflict is on the surface level, where we win and lose, agree and disagree. Unity is down deep, where we understand each other.

Consideration, containment, clarity, and finally *commitment*. This is how the score is kept. I've been told that I shouldn't talk this way because it sounds like a win/lose game, and we should only play win/win games. All right, but still there's something in me that wants to know the score. I want to make sure that when we fight in the church we're keeping track of the things that count in a Christian fight. In the Christian faith and in the Christian church it really doesn't matter what the people down the street think. And it really doesn't matter what my mother wants me to do. What

47

matters is whether I'm into the encounter as a believing, committed, and caring Christian. Because of my Reformed background, I believe that there are three things that really count: the Bible, the Christian tradition, and my personal commitment to Jesus Christ as Lord. If I can't find any support for my opinion in the Bible, then I'd better ask whether I'm on the right side. Or, if I can't find anything in Luther or Calvin or Zwingli or Wesley or the Apostles' Creed or the Sunday school literature or the pronouncements of the General Synod (these are all part of the tradition of the church), then I'd better raise the question about where I'm coming from and what I'm doing. Finally, if I am not willing to take my stand with Christ my brother, I must ask myself if I am being a serious Christian in this encounter.

The issue of conflict and controversy in the church is serious and complex. What I'm working toward is not only a way to understand what's going on, but also a concrete and simple way to begin doing something about it. This simple set of rules and principles is one way to start learning to fight like Christians in the church.

What's Good about the Good Samaritan?

There is a sense in which this is a sermon about Good Samaritans. But in a sense it's not that at all. It's more like a lesson in perception.

It's like this picture which, if you look at it one way, appears to be black faces looking at each other across a white background. Yet, if you look at it another way, it is a white chalice or vase on a black background. What you see depends on which part of the picture you choose to be the foreground and which part of it you choose to be the background. What I have to share with you is the new perception that came to me when a part of the story of the Good Samaritan shifted from the background to the foreground. I saw something I had never seen before. Here is the story:

And behold, a lawyer stood up to put him to the test, saying, "Teacher, what shall I do to inherit eternal life?" He said to him, "What is written in the law? How do you read?" And he answered, "You shall love the Lord your God with all your heart, and with all your soul, and with all your strength, and with all your mind; and your neighbor as yourself." And he said to him, "You have answered right; do this, and you will live." But he, desiring to justify himself, said to Jesus, "And who is my neighbor?"

Jesus replied, "A man was going down from Jerusalem to Jericho, and he fell among robbers, who stripped him and beat him, and departed, leaving him half dead. Now by chance a priest was going down that road; and when he saw him he passed by on the other side. So likewise a Levite, when he came to the place and saw him, passed by on the other side. But a Samaritan, as he journeyed, came to where he was; and when he saw him, he had compassion, and went to him and bound up his wounds, pouring on oil and wine; then he set him on his own beast and brought him to an inn, and took care of him. And the next day he took out two denarii and gave them to the innkeeper, saying, 'Take care of him; and whatever more you spend, I will repay you when I come back.'

Which of these three, do you think, proved neighbor to the man who fell among the robbers?" He said, "The one who showed mercy on him." And Jesus said to him, "Go and do likewise." (Luke 10:25-37)

Notice that this event begins with the lawyer trying to test Jesus. He is not asking the serious question of the rich young man: "What must I do to inherit eternal life?" This is not the cry of the Philippian jailer: "What must I do to be saved?" This is a lawyer asking a tricky question. (How do you handle people who ask you devious questions? Do you give them a serious answer?) Jesus hands it back to the lawyer with: "That's an interesting question, what's *your* answer to it?" Quite predictably he gives a schoolbook answer: "Love the Lord your God," and he quotes the whole thing. Jesus said, "That's fine. You know the answer."

At that point I can just see Jesus turning away. But then the lawyer says, "Wait, I've got one more for you." Luke tells us that the lawyer, "desiring to justify himself," asks Jesus, "And who is my neighbor?" Jesus tells a story, and then at the end he asks, "Now in that story who's the neighbor?" The lawyer replies: "Of course the man who showed compassion."

If I focus on the dialogue between Jesus and the lawyer as the foreground and let the story slip into the background, I see something that I have never seen before. I had usually focused on the story of the Samaritan as the foreground, and the practical question for me was: How can I be a Good Samaritan? When I shift the focus to the dialogue I have a different question to ask. The question in the conversation is,

"Who is my neighbor," and the answer is, "The Good Samaritan." Now my question is, How do I love a Good Samaritan?

I want to deal with that question in a minute. But first I want to deal with what is called a "hermeneutical question." That's a fancy name for a question of scriptural interpretation. The question is: If I now have a new interpretation of this text, what do I do with the other ones I used to believe in?

I used to think that every text in the Bible had just one meaning. In seminary, some teachers encouraged that idea and taught us to peel away everything that lay on top of the text, so we could understand the *one* thing the text meant. Now I've come to understand that the great texts in the Bible are the ones that just keep pumping out meanings, like this story of the Good Samaritan. I now have four different interpretations of that story, and I'm working on a fifth.

I remember that the first one came to me when I was in Sunday school. In those days every Sunday school had Bible pictures on the wall. They were all printed in Providence, Rhode Island, as I recall. The moral of that story for all of us good little boys and girls was that we should be like the Good Samaritan. We should take care of people who get hurt. That's the message I got. So today nobody has to convince me that I ought to have Christian concern for people who are hurt. Nobody has to tell me that world hunger is a high priority issue for Christians. Nobody has to tell me that we ought to be supporting hospitals and homes because I learned as a little child that I should try to be a Good Samaritan.

A second interpretation of that story came to me in adolescence. I discovered that all the people in the world who should have been taking care of me weren't—they were not being Good Samaritans. That was my anti-establishment phase. I felt anger at the Levite who didn't stop to help on his way to the temple. My father was a minister, a super dedicated minister, and I remember a rainy afternoon in the parsonage when my brother and I agreed that our father had time for every kid in town except us. He was like that Levite, in such a rush to get to the temple that he did not have time to stop and care for us poor lonely kids. This interpretation of the story helped me understand myself during a very important period in my growing up.

When I got caught up in the civil rights movement I was reminded that Samaritans were to Jews in Jesus' time what Blacks are to Anglo-Saxon Protestants in our time, and this helped me get in touch with some of my prejudices. As a card-carrying yankee liberal living in Nashville, Tennessee, I found plenty of occasions to preach to my southern brethren on this text using this third interpretation!

A fourth meaning for the story helped me understand myself when I moved to Lancaster, Pennsylvania. Having spent fifteen years trying to figure out Southern Baptists, and other church people down South, I now found myself among Pennsylvania-German folk. I was eager to understand my new friends and colleagues. So, since preachers are my favorite people, and finding out what they're doing is my favorite hobby, I started meeting with groups of ministers. Many of these Lutheran, United Presbyterian, United Church of Christ, and United Methodist pastors that I met were worried about what they called

53

"fundamentalists." For fifteen years I had lived where fundamentalism was the established religion. In Tennessee, Presbyterians and Lutherans were considered odd, and there were almost no United Church of Christ congregations. So I asked: "What do you mean by fundamentalists?" They answered without hesitation: "You know, those Bible people, those charismatics, those Pentecostals, people like that." They were lumping together as fundamentalist a lot of people I considered to be quite different from one another. So I asked myself, "What is their problem? Why are they so uptight? Why are they so angry? Why are they so frightened?" It came to me, after about six months of hearing this complaint over and over again, that I could identify with their feeling because I had that same feeling.

Most of us had come into the ministry in a generation when we knew we were ministers when we were helping people. If you wanted to be taken under care of some ecclesiastical body as a candidate for the ministry, the one thing that turned them on was a young person who "wanted to help people." In my own ministry I felt very much like a minister when I was "helping people." That meant that I tended to orient myself primarily toward helpless people. I didn't know what to do with people unless they were helpless. If they had a question, I had an answer. If they were weak, I could bring them strength. If they were lost, I could show them the way. If they were confused, I could give them coherence and clarity. But if somebody came to me who had it all together, I wouldn't know what to do. They weren't asking for help. What did I have to give them?

On one of those days when I was trying to understand this question of weakness and strength in my own ministry, I was asked to preach on the lectionary lesson for the coming Sunday. It was Luke 10:25-27—the story of the Good Samaritan. "Ho hum," I thought to myself, "I'll get my Good Samaritan sermon out of the barrel and preach it again." But I reached for my Bible before I reached for my barrel, and God used that story to open my eyes to something I needed to learn about myself. As I read the text, the story slipped into the background, and the conversation between Jesus and the lawyer moved into the foreground. And there it was—a new meaning for me. Who is my neighbor? Who am I to love and to serve? I am to love and serve the Good Samaritan. And who is the Good Samaritan? He's the one who already understands the gospel. She's the one already doing acts of mercy. He's already spending his own money to take care of the needy. She doesn't need me. She knows what to do. He knows how to do it, and he's doing it. But how can I love someone I can't help?

There's something in me that doesn't want to hear this fifth interpretation because I have always had trouble receiving affection and attention. I'm embarrassed when people treat me with compassion. I have difficulty accepting help. I find it easier to love people who need me. If I can do something for you, then I feel strong and whole and well and capable. I like to feel strong and whole and well and capable. So I may even find myself helping you in ways that keep you needy and dependent, because it meets my need to be strong and capable. But if I let myself be helped, I am forced to confront my own weakness, my own need, my own

55

feelings of helplessness, and most of the time I don't like to do this. Usually I find ways to protect myself against these feelings by being helpful. Who is my neighbor? If it's the Good Samaritans, then maybe I'm the one in the ditch? I must learn to let them help me—and love them for doing so.

Now, all the other interpretations are still meaningful to me. There's still something in me that wants to be a Good Samaritan, and I will find somebody to help—one way or another. The Bible picture on the Sunday school wall is still part of me. I'll take care of something, even if it's only a lost puppy or a bird with a broken wing. And I'll find a way, in the name of compassion, to stand against the establishment, institutional indifference, and welfare programs that demean—and all those other Levites and priests who pass by on the other side. I'll continue to get in touch with the deep-seated prejudices in myself and other people and understand more about how they obscure and distort human relations and social systems.

I'm not exactly clear about everything that my fifth interpretation means. It's more clue than conclusion. But it has taught me something about who my neighbor is and how to love him and her. So I'll add it to my collection of interpretations and use it until the next one comes along. And I hope some of these perceptions will focus for you what's good about the Good Samaritan.

V.

Lord, Teach Us to Pray

(Psalm 19:1-4, 14. Luke 11:1-13)

I want to reflect with you on the two sides of prayer—speaking and listening, words and silence. Here is the text which sets the theme and provides the title for this sermon.

"He was praying in a certain place, and when he ceased one of his disciples said to him, "Lord, teach us to pray" (Luke 11:1).

This text is pleasing to the practical theologian in me because the request is practical. The disciples asked for teaching, and Jesus taught them. But what are we taught in this text? First, we learn that the idea of prayer is caught before it is taught. The disciples saw Jesus doing something, and they wanted to learn how to do it. He was caught in the act, and they wanted to get into the act. Secondly, what they saw him doing was talking to his Father, and they wanted to learn how to begin their own conversations. This is a picture of prayer as a relationship to God which takes the form of words. Learning to pray, therefore, is something like learning to talk.

The words he gave them were simple words. The first word was a name—"Abba," which means Father. Scholars tell us that this is Aramaic baby talk. In some countries babies say Pappa and Dadda. But Jewish babies in Palestine during the first century evidently said Abba. Even Paul, who was not given to simple thoughts, understood the meaning of this word.

For all who are led by the Spirit of God are sons of God. For you did not receive the spirit of slavery to fall back into fear, but you received the spirit of sonship. When we cry, "Abba! Father!" it is the Spirit himself bearing witness with our spirit that we are children of God. (Romans 8:14-16)

Abba, Father, are the words to say. And yet they are not just words. They are the sign of a relationship. It is the relationship we seek, and not the words. Yet it takes the form of words. On the speaking side, the mystery of prayer is summed up in a psalm: "Let the words of my mouth and the meditation of my heart be acceptable in thy sight" (19:14). So how do I ever find the words that speak the meditation of my heart? How do I ever find a way to express what is inside me with words that are outside me? Jesus suggests that we be wary of words.

And in praying do not heap up empty phrases as the Gentiles do; for they think they will be heard for their many words. Do not be like them, for your Father knows what you need before you ask him. (Matthew 6:7-8)

I expected him to say, "Some people think they're going to be heard for their words so don't worry about your words. Words don't count." But instead he says, "When you pray this is the way: 'Our Father who art in heaven. . . ' " Isn't it strange that he says, in effect, "Don't think you're going to be heard because of your words, but when you pray be sure to say these words." Like so many things in the Bible, it doesn't make sense at first. It doesn't follow logically. It takes us by surprise. But let us take the text as it is, and ask what it can mean.

The mystery of the relationship between prayer and the words of one's prayer continues to fascinate me. I am reminded of a Sunday in one of the little churches in Greene County, Tennessee, where I had been sent by the Board of National Missions of the United Presbyterian Church. The synod executive had given me an assignment: "Make Presbyterians out of those people. They've been Baptists long enough!" This meant that I was to get them to sing out of the *Hymnal* and have the Session keep proper records and do everything decently and in order. It also meant that I was supposed to lead the Sunday service out of *The Book of Common Worship.* And that's what I did on my first Sunday in the parish. After the service one of the elders met me at the door, looked me squarely in the eye, and said: "Young man, as far as I'm concerned a prayer read out of a book doesn't get through the ceiling." (Up to that time I had never really reckoned with the ceiling-piercing power of my prayers!)

So at the next meeting of the Session I called on that brother to pray. Under my breath I was saying, "Okay fella, you don't like the way I do it, you do it." Without a moment's hesitation he rose to his feet, closed his eyes, threw back his head, and said in effect: "Lord we thank you for bringing us here to do the work of the church. Guide us by your spirit to do all things according to thy will. Forgive us of our sins for Jesus' sake. Amen." Then he sat down. And I thought to myself: When I get to where I can pray like that, I won't need a prayer book.

59

So at the next meeting of the Session I called on the brother to pray again. He didn't hesitate for a minute. He hopped up, closed his eyes, threw back his head, and said in effect: "Lord we thank you for bringing us here tonight to do the work of the church. Lead us by your spirit to do all things according to thy will. Forgive us of our sins for Jesus' sake. Amen." And he sat down. Right then I knew it didn't matter whether our prayers were written down, from a book, or tattooed on the back of our eyelids so that everytime we closed our eyes we could just read them off. Somewhere along the way we learn to pray by overhearing prayer words, then learning them, and speaking them. Sometimes they get to be just words and are no longer prayers. Yet always we search for the words that are truly a prayer for us, as we struggle to learn to pray.

I remember another time, back when our older children were in Sunday school, and our youngest daughter was still too young to go. It was our custom at mealtime to hold hands around the table and say a prayer. One evening she said, "I want to say my prayer." Her older brother, as older brothers will, said, "You don't know one." "Yes, I do!" she insisted. So we all held hands and bowed our heads, waiting. Very solemnly she said: "I pledge allegiance to the flag of the United States . . ." Of course we all broke up! What had happened? Although she hadn't been to Sunday school, she had watched *Romper Room* on television. That was her "school." The program began every morning with all the little children getting very solemn, dropping their voices a little, and saying the Pledge to the Flag. To her it *sounded* like the words we said when we were praying. How was she to know? Are any solemn, seriously spoken words a prayer? We learn how to pray. We struggle for the words and sometimes find them.

What I've learned in struggling to pray is that the words are for *us,* and not for God. We are not heard by our speaking, but our speaking is heard. *We* hear the speaking. My words reveal something of the meditation of my heart that I would not otherwise hear unless I speak the words. I struggle to turn outward something that is inward, and at the same time, to take something that is outward and turn it inward. I still find that when I cannot pray with my own words, I turn to the "prayer words" I have learned. Sometimes I have no prayer at night except—"Now I lay me down to sleep . . ." Sometimes that is still my best prayer. Maybe I should have outgrown it, gone beyond it, and yet I've learned that I never do leave it behind. It's always there for me, just like the Lord's Prayer. This is really a very subtle and mysterious thing. One of the wisest statements I know of is by Samuel Miller. In the following passage he is speaking about church architecture, but what he says helps me understand my prayers.

There is a sense in which the church comes out of history and into our lives laden with doctrines and teachings, with great buildings and ecclesiastical traditions, and we accept it or reject it, but there is another sense in which the church comes out of us and goes into history. You and I take what we are inside ourselves and make of it this outer sanctuary beautified with our grace of soul or made ugly with our ineptitude and stupidity.

In the Middle Ages men built cathedrals of such enduring grandeur that now we look back on them with wonder. It was such an age of ignorance, of darkness and superstition so we think, and yet in that time the souls of men turned inside out, fashioned magnificent cathedrals to pierce the sky and stand century after century like enduring beacons of spiritual truth in the swirling tides of the world. Perhaps it was not as dark or ignorant or stupid a time as we have thought. Certainly in our day when we have turned our souls inside out and made churches for them we built some very strange and squalid things: auditoriums, lyceums, gymnasiums, but not the kind of places where the souls of man could appropriately kneel or meet the wonder of the everlasting God or see the beauty of his holiness reflected in the thing dedicated to his use.

Here in this place we read the signs and symbols not of ancient history, though all of things have happened somewhere sometime. We read the signs and symbols of our life until we see that these things pictured in glass, molded in stone, fashioned in wood first came out of our experience of life. We shall not know ourselves or the church, no we shall not know Christ or the Gospel or the Bible until turning from this outer world we identify the originals in ourselves in our birth, in growth, in our sin, in our lost innocence, in the cross we bear in our humanity, and in the death we must someday suffer. This building is the solid shadow of our spirit. We build it with wood and stone, with hands of flesh but the reality of this place existed first within us. If this thing we have made is ugly it can be said with certainty that what it came from in the souls of men is ugly too, or if this thing is made with beauty then that out of which it came must have had the beauty of holiness and the grace of God upon it. (*The Life of the Church,* Harper, 1953, pp. 64–65)

This passage helps me understand how the words of my prayer are for me. They are an attempt to bring outward, in audible form, what I take to be an inner mystery in my own life. In speaking and hearing those words I confront the holiness or the ugliness, the love or the hate, as it comes out of me.

I am reminded of another occasion when I was praying with the choir of a congregation. I was praying the kind of prayer that pastors pray with choirs before the service. "O Lord, go with us into this service and confirm our gifts as we sing and preach that these thy people may worship thee in spirit and in truth." I was saying in effect: "O Lord go with us . . . I've got my sermon outlined, the choir has memorized the anthem, now come along and bless all this." I realized that so often I get up in the morning and say, "OK Lord, I have it all planned, just help me get through it." Seldom do I say, "All right Lord, what's up today? What would you have me do?" My words convict me of my arrogance. And these words are for me. So in prayer, we seek to find words that speak the meaning of our lives, the meditations of our hearts. We seek to find ways of speaking that relate us to God using the vocabulary of prayer.

But that's only half the story. For if prayer is that part of our relationship with God which is like a conversation, it is not just a question of how we talk, but also how we listen. It is not just a question of whether God is listening and whether we can learn to *speak* so that he hears us, but whether God is speaking and whether we can learn to *listen* so that we hear him. What do you believe? Do you believe that God is listening and that therefore it is worth your struggle to try to speak? Do you believe that God is speaking and that therefore it is worth your struggle to try to listen? One of the above, both of the above, none of the above? To get hold of this let's turn to an Old Testament story. It's a short one, so I'll quote it just as it is in the Bible.

Now the boy Samuel was ministering to the Lord under Eli. And the word of the Lord was rare in those days; there was no frequent vision.

At that time Eli, whose eyesight had begun to grow dim, so that he could not see, was lying in his own place; the lamp of God had not yet gone out, and Samuel was lying down within the temple of the Lord, where the ark of God was. Then the Lord called, "Samuel! Samuel!" and he said, "Here I am!" and ran to Eli, and said, "Here I am, for you called me." But he said, "I did not call; lie down again." So he went and lay down. And the Lord called again, "Samuel!" And Samuel arose and went to Eli, and said, "Here I am, for you called me." But he said, "I did not call, my son; lie down again." Now Samuel did not yet know the Lord, and the word of the Lord had not yet been revealed to him. And the Lord called Samuel again the third time. And he arose and went to Eli, and said, "Here I am, for you called me." Then Eli perceived that the Lord was calling the boy. Therefore Eli said to Samuel, "Go, lie down; and if he calls you, you say, 'Speak Lord, for thy servant hears.' " So Samuel went and lay down in his place.

And the Lord came and stood forth, calling as at other times, "Samuel! Samuel!" And Samuel said, "Speak, for thy servant hears." (I Samuel 3:1-10)

Fascinating story! I remember it from my days as a child in the church. This is one of the stories that I grew up on, one of the stories that I thought I understood as a child. Now I see a lot more in it. Let's look at it to see what we can learn about the listening side of prayer.

"The word of the Lord was rare in those days. There was no frequent vision." That is to say, nobody was expecting to hear anything, nobody was expecting to see anything. There wasn't any point in listening because there was nothing to listen for. This was the tradition in which Samuel was growing up. There was a lot to do down at the temple—keep the lights burning and sleep by the ark, sweep the place out in the morning and clean up after the pigeons. All that sort of thing. Then one night a curious thing happened. Samuel knew who to go to when somebody called. He knew who gave the orders around there. He didn't know that there was anything else. Three times he goes to Eli. Finally Eli realizes what is going on, and tells Samuel what to do—simply say, "Here I am. Speak Lord, I'm listening." He gave him words to say.

I didn't quote beyond verse ten because the message that the Lord had for Samuel was a dreadful and terrifying message. The message, you may remember, is that Eli and his sons are going to be killed because they have been faithless. What an awful thing to lay on a child. What a frightening thing to hear in the night. Well, you can look this story up another time. Just remember that this event is part of a larger setting. There's more to the story than simply praying and piety; it has to do with the whole question of justice and righteousness, and holiness and truth within the nation. But in the midst of all that there are times and moments when the best thing for us to do is to listen. This story teaches me first of all that I must learn how to listen, how to be quiet.

There is another clue in Mark's Gospel. And he said to them, "Is a lamp brought in to be put under a bushel, or under a bed, and not on a stand? For there is nothing hid except to be made manifest; nor anything secret, except to come to light. If any man has ears to hear, let him hear" (4:21-23).

And then this curious phrase:

And he said to them, "Take heed to what you hear; the measure you give will be the measure you get, and still more will be given you. For to him who has will more be given; and from him who has not, even that will be taken away." (24-25)

"Listen to what you hear," he is saying. Sounds obvious, but the point is that there is no shortage of messages. God is speaking everywhere. If we will stop and be still, we will hear something. Will we listen? Can we listen? How do we listen?

"Listen carefully to what you already hear." There's already so much going on that I do not hear. Have you ever had the experience of going out into the woods at night, far from any signs of civilization, and being aware all of a sudden of how terribly quiet it is? Then, if you stay longer and become quieter, you become aware of how much noise there is in the silence: the birds, the creek, the squeaks, the chatters. Having been stilled by the silence, I become even more stilled, and I am aware that I am hearing things that I wasn't listening for. Much of the noise I hear is of my own making. I fill the silence with a lot of my own static. I have trouble turning off the chatter partly because I'm so verbally oriented (that's a fancy way of saying I talk a lot). I'm still trying to find the way to "be still and know." It's hard for me to turn off my mouth—to be still—to be quiet. But I'm learning.

I think it is instructive that God comes to Samuel when he's lying down, about to go to sleep. His first reaction is to get up and do something, to rush somewhere and talk to somebody. But Eli knows better, and he says, "Go back and lie down, be still, keep quiet. If it happens again don't be worried about what you're going to say. Be interested in what you're hearing. Listen to what you already hear." Samuel had been hearing, but he hadn't been listening. In God's voice he had heard the sound of Eli. Eli says in effect, "Listen to what you hear, and maybe you'll hear the difference."

Another thing I learn from this story is that it is often helpful to take the advice of others. Other people have been along the same path and know something of the way. Although Eli had been an unfaithful priest, he was nonetheless able to minister to this child and show him the way. I have gotten help from many people who have shared with me their experiences and their words, their nuts and bolts, their ways to be quiet and to listen. One who has been most helpful is Henry Nouwen, a Dutch Roman Catholic priest who teaches at Yale Divinity School. He writes simply and forcefully about the spiritual life. I recommend all his books, especially one called *Reaching Out: The Three Dimensions of the Spiritual Life*.

My own path to prayer has been very gradual. I grew up in the church surrounded by praying and learned to pray in public. But I discovered about five years ago that I had never learned to pray by myself. I don't know how I escaped. I don't know how I survived. I'd been a Christian for over fifty years and an ordained clergy person for twenty-five of those years, but I had not sought to be a person of prayer. When I began to want to pray but didn't know how, I didn't know whom to ask for help. In desperation I turned to a friend who happened to be a Roman Catholic priest. He helped me, and I began to learn to pray. In the life of prayer I

67

consider myself about four and a half years old. I'm somewhere between crawling and walking. I'm no spiritual athlete. I have very little to say. But so far I have learned three things.

First, there are prayer words all around me, residues of the prayers of others, words which are here for me to learn and use. When the disciples asked, "Lord, teach us to pray," Jesus taught them a prayer. That was a way of beginning. I've learned that I can rely on this prayer. I've also learned that these words are not just my words. They are the treasures of the Christian community. Part of the mystery and struggle of my life is to find my own words for the meditations of my heart. It is a struggle in which I grow.

Second, learning the words of prayer is important, but it's only half of the story. The other half is learning to be still and to listen. For me that's been the hardest part. So several times a year I go to special places for retreats.

Third, I've learned to accept the direction of others who are on the way. They may not be any better than I am, or even much farther along, but they all have something to teach me. And the miracle is that they are willing to take the time to pray with me and for me! They are an answer to prayer.

At the beginning, the place to begin to pray is with the prayer: "Lord, teach us to pray." As Jesus taught them, he teaches us to

begin with baby talk	"Abba, Father . . ."
soar to spiritual heights	"in heaven, hallowed . . ."
seek his kingdom	"thy kingdom come . . ."
be down to earth	"on earth . . ."

ask for the ordinary	"give us daily bread . . ."
face our sin	"forgive us . . ."
bind ourselves to our	
brothers and sisters	"as we forgive . . ."
confess our fears	"lead us not . . ."
pray for liberation	"deliver us . . ."
praise him	"thine is the glory . . ."

And as we grow in the life of prayer, we find that God is answering that first, faint prayer of our hearts: "Lord, teach us to pray."

VI.

Don't Put Your Patch on My Wineskin

(Deuteronomy 30:11-14. Matthew 9:10-17)

"What do you want to be when you grow up?" she asked. "I want to be a bigger me," the child replied.

I wish I'd thought of that. But I grew up in a time when that wasn't the thing to say. You had to "become something," you had to "make something of yourself" —as if being me wasn't all right. So I learned to say what was expected. "I want to be a _____," depending on who was asking. I didn't deal with my identity. I just identified myself with some occupation or group—and that was it. They left me alone. I didn't let it bother me too much—yet I aways envied people who "knew what they wanted to be." But I like to say—I really don't know what I want to be when I grow up—because that's pretty much how I feel these days. I've discovered how much energy it takes to be what I am. There isn't a lot left over to become something else. I commented earlier on the dangers of "negative identity." So now I am trying to understand identity as a positive and personal thing.

Identity questions affect individuals and institutions. For institutions the question might be how to retain diversity and pluralism and still sustain some sense of common life and mission. For individuals it could be how to hold on to what we know is good even though it's old, and how to reach out and draw into ourselves what is new even though we aren't sure that it is good. Identity questions revolve around our beliefs about what is good and bad in the old and the new. We see ourselves most clearly when relationships and events show us how we are changing and not changing. I find that returning to the scriptures provides an occasion for touching base with the old and for testing the new. So I suggest the following text. "And no one puts a piece of unshrunk cloth on an old garment, for the patch tears away from the garment, and a worse tear is made. Neither is new wine put into old wineskins, if it is, the skins burst, and the wine is spilled, and the skins are destroyed; but new wine is put into fresh wineskins, and so both are preserved" (Matthew 9:16-17).

What we have here in these words of Jesus are homely references to common, ordinary, everyday things that people understand. Jesus seldom started with abstract theological or religious propositions and then tried to illustrate them in the manner of some preachers. Rather, he pointed to ordinary things and asked us to look for the deeper meaning in them. That's what I want us to do with this text. What can we make of patches on garments or wine in wineskins? I see some similarities between patches and wineskins and between being middle-aged and the meaning of true conservatism. Because of my religious upbringing I know more about patches on garments than I know about wine and wineskins. And because of my professional training I know more about being a liberal than a conservative. And I certainly know a lot about being middle-aged!

Remember that Jesus was speaking primarily to poor people. They were the ones who heard him gladly. He spoke to them of things they knew. Patches. They had

71

to patch their garments. They couldn't afford school clothes and work clothes and Sunday clothes. They had to make do with what they had. The process of patching and mending and making do was a daily struggle they understood. Wine and wineskins. The poor people couldn't afford new wineskins every year. They had to do the best they could with some old skins which had become hard and parched, brittle and stiff. Not being able to afford new wineskins they had to find a way to soften and freshen the old ones so that they could use them once again.

We know something about patches in our modern households where our sons and daughters pride themselves on blue jeans that are many years old. They consist mostly of patches. There are patches on the patches and embroidery on top of that. I've watched this process, and I've seen what happens when you take an old pair of faded blue jeans and put a bright new patch on them. It doesn't work. Something must give in the fibers of the new patch. The patch must be shrunk before it's put on or it will tear loose—and make a bigger hole. It's all a question of "fit."

Then there's the wine and the wineskins. A simple exegesis of the text suggests that poor folk didn't have new skins every year so they had to soak and soften and freshen the old ones so they'd be flexible. When new wine is put in a wineskin it has to bubble up for a time before it settles down. If the wineskin can't stretch it simply breaks. The skin is broken, and the wine is also lost. Everything is lost. In these two cases the new and the old have to find a way to fit together or they are both lost. If both parts of a relationship seek to remain unchanged, then the relationship has no future.

But only one part has to change to make things fit.

This is what I've learned about relationships. When two people are having trouble, only one has to change to correct the relationship. The one who *can* is the one who *must*. Take the patch on the garment. The faded blue jeans are old and have shrunk all they can shrink. They can't be shrunk any more. But the new material can. The new material still has the ability to change. If it will allow itself to be changed, it can fit the one that cannot change. If a person insists on being what he or she is with no regard for what the other person is, the relationship is strained, torn, destroyed. So it is in many relationships that those of us who are young and a little more flexible are the ones who must change, because we are the ones who can. Those who are older may not have to change because sometimes they can't.

I met a man recently who told me two things. One, he's eighty years old. Two, he had a new idea and changed his mind about something important. I know that being old and being young are not simply a function of chronological age—we just label each other that way. Personally, I feel a whole lot more flexible now that I'm over fifty than when I was under forty. I have paid my dues, and I don't have to be so up tight anymore. There's a tremendous freedom which comes when you've paid your dues. Whatever the chronological age, the dynamics are the same. Somebody is a little more flexible than somebody else, and so when flexibility is required the one who has it can use it. Both people don't have to stretch because either one can make the relationship fit. It's the same thing with the wine and the wineskins. You have the picture of an old wineskin which is stiff and rigid and hard, but it can be changed. It can be dampened and softened and kneaded and worked until it becomes flexible. New wine is different. It's just coming to life. It can't stop bubbling. It has no control over itself. In this case it's the new wine that can't change. So the old wineskins have to be flexible, they must soften to accommodate the bubbling enthusiasm of youth lest it be lost. The truth is the same with patches, but in reverse. If neither changes, both are lost. Only one must change to save them both. That's the meaning of true conservatism: saving both.

This leads me to some observations about what I consider to be the special ministry of the middle-aged. Those of us who are neither old nor young have been given a special, temporary gift from God. I am just old enough to understand and appreciate the values of the older generation, and just young enough to appreciate and value the rising expectations of the new generation. Some of my friends, who are a little younger than I am, cannot see any good in the old. Others, who are just a little older, cannot see value in what is new. But some of us find in being middle-aged the possibility of a ministry between the generations. It is a ministry that holds together patches and garments, wine and wineskins. It's a maintenance ministry. It doesn't look very creative. But its purpose is to conserve the best in both. And that's an important ministry.

In trying to understand the nature of conservatism, I have identified three Christian life-styles: the rebel, the revolutionary, and the radical. I remember my life as a *rebel* when I affirmed myself by kicking other people and institutions. I kicked the church until my foot got sore. I thought I knew who I was because I knew what I was against. But nothing changed.

Then I became a *revolutionary*. I sought to improve my place in life by changing things around me so that the world would be a better place for me to live in. I thought I could improve my character if only the world would change. I had something in mind for everybody else. I wanted them to change their lives so that my life would then be more like I wanted it to be. So I went through that revolutionary stage, and the world changed, but I didn't feel much better.

Now I'm learning what it means to be a *radical*. This word comes from the same term as "radish" which means "root." Radicals have to do with roots. I'm now trying to be more radical, to find out what changes in myself will allow me to grow as I want to be. If these changes in me initiate changes outside myself, that is fine. As I focus on changing myself, I am learning that unless and until I assume responsibility for myself, I have not yet done anything important.

A radical life-style is a model of integrity for those of us who have made commitments to relationships, to communities, and to institutions and are still committed to liberation, life, and growth. But the radical Christian life-style is also conservative in the traditional sense because it does not always lead us to choose the new over the old or vice versa. The true conservative would save everything that is good. As Paul says, "Hold fast to what is good." Not "hold fast to everything you've got," but "hold fast to what is good." Some of the good is old, and some of the good is new. Some of it is forgotten and some of it is yet to be, but the true conservative seeks to save all that is good, all that can be saved.

I used to believe there were two kinds of people in the world: the liberals and the conservatives—people like me and all those other closed-minded folk. I don't believe that anymore because both of these mind-sets describe me and everybody else I've ever met. There's something in me that wants to hold on to what is familiar and precious, but that bores me. There's something in me that wants to reach out to what is new and exciting and challenging, but that frightens me. So I move back and forth between the two. When I come into a relationship with another person who is up tight about something that I'm not very worried about, they look very conservative and I feel very liberal. In another case I may be faced with giving up something that I really care about, something in which the other person has little self-investment. Then I feel very conservative, and they look very liberal. Or, I may go to one church meeting and feel like the most liberal person in the group. But then at another meeting I may feel like the most conservative. I haven't changed. There are always relationships in my life that put me in touch with parts of myself that are closed and stiff and rigid, but these same relationships also bring out parts of me that are open, questing, and searching. I'm neither one nor the other. I'm both. This makes me a radical and a conservative—all at the same time. I like that.

So I'm now looking for ways to hold things together: patches on garments, wine in wineskins, old and new, young and old, parents and children, pastors and lay people. In all these relationships we can find the best in each other and hold on to it together. In changing times when it's hard to know what to do, it takes all the prayer and patience we have. But as I say, don't try to put your patch on my wineskin. Let's work out our relationship together. God wants it that way.

VII.

Feasting or Fasting?

A Seasonal Sermon for Lent

(Ecclesiastes 3:1-8. Matthew 9:10-15)

I want to share some of what it means to me to celebrate Lent—to enter into it, to keep it. And I do this as one who was raised in a tradition where we didn't do things like that. Lent was something that Catholics did, and that meant we didn't. We didn't know why they *did,* but that meant we *didn't.* I was dimly aware that there was some talk about Lent among Episcopalians and Catholics, and that they "gave up things for Lent." In those days Lent was no part of my life. But now it is becoming a significant season for me.

Lent is a time to take care of myself, a time for reflection, for self-examination, for recollection. One of the things I need during Lent is a discipline, a focus for my reflection. So for our reflection I offer two familiar texts. The first is a poem from the book of Ecclesiastes,

For everything there is a season,
  and a time for every matter under heaven:
A time to be born, and a time to die;
A time to plant, and a time to pluck up what is planted; . . .
A time to keep silent, and a time to speak; . . . (3:1-2, 7)

I am sure you know this poem. I commend it to you for regular reflection.

The second focus is an event in Jesus' life from the Gospel of Matthew:

And as he sat at table in the house, behold, many tax collectors and sinners came and sat down with Jesus and his disciples. And when the Pharisees saw this, they said to his disciples, "Why does your teacher eat with tax collectors and sinners?" But when he heard it, he said, "Those who are well have no need of a physician, but those who are sick. Go and learn what this means, 'I desire mercy, and not sacrifice.' For I came not to call the righteous, but sinners." Then the disciples of John came to him, saying, "Why do we and the Pharisees fast, but your disciples do not fast?" And Jesus said to them, "Can the wedding guests mourn as long as the bridegroom is with them? The days will come, when the bridegroom is taken away from them, and then they will fast." (9:10-15)

Lent is a special time, but what kind of time is it? What kind of celebration shall it be? With what attitudes and expectations shall we enter into it? Is it more like a wedding or a funeral? Is it a time to remember a death, or to prepare for a resurrection? Is it a time for fasting, or a time for feasting? Which is it? The answer, of course, is yes.

We are sometimes told that Lent is a time when we should be serious and solemn, when we should practice self-examination and inquire into our shame and guilt, a time when we should withdraw and be ourselves, a time for quiet and thoughtful reflection. There are also suggestions that this is a season for us to be spontaneous and joyful, to count our blessings, to be with one another, to go about not with heads bowed but with heads up. In the two texts I find both of these moods. John's disciples are observing that Jesus and his disciples are not as solemn and glum as they are. "Why is it that we fast but you do not?" I want to get back to that in a minute. But first of all I would like to digress here and deal with the kind of question that is being asked.

I learned recently that "why" questions are often not questions at all. When somebody says to me, "Why are you doing that?" I suspect that they don't really want to know why at all—they just want me to stop. "Why are you doing that?" is not really a question. It is a challenge. I have observed that often the answer to the apparent question "Why are you doing that?" is the apparent question "Why not?" This is not an exchange of questions, but a challenge and a defense. So when John's disciples came and asked, "Why do we fast and you don't?" I don't think they really wanted to know why Jesus wasn't fasting, they were telling him he should! Jesus does not respond with "why not?" but with a real question. He asks them, "Can the wedding guests mourn as long as the bridegroom is with them? The days will come, when the bridegroom is taken away from them, and then they will fast." His response is a clue to how we ought to behave in keeping Lent. Should we fast, be solemn and serious, or should we feast, be jolly and happy? The answer, of course, is yes. Both are appropriate.

Here Jesus suggests that the issue is appropriateness. He says, "Yes, there is a time for being jolly, and a time for being solemn. There are wedding feasts and there are funerals." What are we doing during Lent? Are we coming to a wedding feast or to a funeral? The season includes both. It includes Good Friday (which is funereal) and Easter (which is festive). As Ecclesiastes says, "There is a time to weep and a time to laugh. A time to mourn and a time to dance." There is a rhythm in life. Life moves between two poles and stretches us. A black spiritual puts it another way: "Sometimes I'm up, sometimes I'm down. Oh, Yes, Lord!" The point is to say yes to both.

Keeping the festivals of the Christian year doesn't seem very risky because we always know how they will come out, don't we? So during Advent it's very hard for us to act like we are ancient Israelites wondering if the Messiah will come; because we've already read the Book, we know how the story ends. There's no point in faking it, or in acting out something we already have the answer to. We don't need to worry about how the story comes out. That's not the question. The question is how are *we* going to come through it?

The question during Lent is for us. Can *we* enter deeply into the wrestling and struggling of our Lord with his mission and his ministry? Will we die enough during these days of Lent so that we come to Easter with new life? Do we think we can prove we are pious by playing a game? Or do we use the season to prove the power of God to change our lives? Jesus suggests that when it comes to deciding how to celebrate there are three things to consider: the nature of the occasion; the people who are part of it; and what behavior is appropriate for the particular people participating. First, the nature of the occasion. A wedding feast, when the bridegroom is with you, is a happy time. A funeral is not a party, it is a time for solemnity and fasting. The occasion sets the mood and has its own purposes and parameters. There are customs and traditions.

But the occasion is also affected by the people who are there and what it means to them. I've been to wedding parties where some people weren't happy. The fellow who didn't get the girl, and the parents who weren't sure they got the right son-in-law. (They say behind every successful man is a surprised mother-in-law.) And I've been to some funerals where there were some happy people, happy because a loved one had been released from a painful illness. There was sadness, but also a kind of joy. Others have been surprised and shocked and struck down by sudden loss. Again, it's not just the occasion but the way in which people come to the occasion and how the occasion and the person come together.

During Lent there is a tradition, and a pattern. It is usually a time for increased devotion and daily prayer. There is a turning inward in search of silence and centering. It is also a time for turning outward in service and sacrifice. The Lenten Offering, which links personal self-denial with reaching out to the world's poor, combines the two. But as Jesus said, "The days will come, when the bridegroom is taken away from them, and then they will fast." Times change.

What kind of occasion, then, is Lent, and who are we, and how will it be for us? What I want to suggest is that we say yes to everything, that we not choose or decide in advance what kind of time it will be as if we could set our mood and control our life so that we will always "do the right thing." Rather, let us ask who we are as we come, and let us come as we are into the days of Lent—weeping and laughing, giving thanks and begging forgiveness. Let us ask how faithful we have been as servants of Jesus Christ and rejoice in the memory of those times when we have indeed walked in faith.

For some of us Christ is close and dear and strong right now. It is therefore appropriate for us to rejoice, to savor that presence as with the bridegroom at the wedding feast, and to want to sing and dance and testify and share. But for some of us Christ is not real and strong and clear. He seems distant and puzzling, even frightening. When the bridegroom has been taken away, we do not feel like singing and dancing. We feel like weeping and begging. And if that's how we feel—then that's how we should act. What God gives us in the days of Lent is a chance to be who we are in his presence and to know that we are accepted just as we are. There is not one thing we have to do or say to qualify for God's grace. Whether we are up or down we can claim the promise that God is with us always. God calls us to come, to taste, and to see.

So we enter into Lent, a traditional period of forty days. Officially it starts on Ash Wednesday when some people go to church and have ashes put on their faces. It is a very solemn moment. Yet in the Anglican Prayerbook, the text for that service is the one from Matthew which warns against praying in public and being seen by men, and advises going into your room and shutting the door (6:5-6). It also says, in effect, "When you fast, do not put ashes on your face, but wash your face and go out with a smile" (6:16-18). There is a beautiful irony in it. On Ash Wednesday, when in solemnity we come to have ashes put on our faces, the text is warning us not to take this too seriously because if we think that by doing something outward we are doing something inward, we are just fooling ourselves. So let us try every way we can, outward and inward, with and without ashes, with and without songs, with and without words, together and alone, to claim the ancient promise of renewal during the days of Lent.

I pray that in these days each of us will come closer to God by coming closer to ourselves. Not feeling that we have to act in a certain way in order to qualify, to be correct, or to "do it right"—but that as we open our lives to the leading of God's Spirit, to God's grace and judgment, we shall come to see what kind of occasion this is for us. Is it a time for feasting or a time for fasting? The answer, of course, is yes. It depends on who you are and where you are in relation to your own commitments and to the claim of God on your life. And I pray that there will be, during Lent and all your days, some feasting, some fasting, some joy, some sorrow. Some simplifying of your life toward its center, some stretching of your life to the limits of your possibilities—so that as our lives open up to Easter it may be a new kind of life—for each of us and all of us.

Selfishness, Service, and Sacrifice

(I Kings 3:5-13. Matthew 20:17-28)

On February 7, 1978, Dr. James D. Smart of Toronto, Canada, gave a lecture at a Lancaster Seminary convocation entitled "The Bible and the Pulpit." I have known and respected Dr. Smart for many years as a distinguished scholar and powerful advocate of biblically based Christian education in the local church. He had lectured once before at Lancaster Seminary in the early 70s, and so I was pleased and proud to have him return to our campus to share some of his concerns and commitments in relation to the Bible and the church. He made a powerful address which affected me very deeply. It happened that it was my responsibility to preach in seminary chapel the very next day. I had not intended to respond to his address, but as I prepared for the occasion, I found myself dealing with some of the things he had said.

What follows is transcribed from a tape made by Barbara Brummet, one of my students. I want to leave this sermon pretty much as is. It contains my immediate response to a particular situation which illustrates what I have said in the Prologue about my preaching. I never prepare general sermons, but always preach to a particular occasion. I have a feeling that the ideas in this sermon are going to be developed more generally as I use the same material in other

84

settings. But I wanted to include one sermon pretty much in its original form to illustrate what I say about "prophetic preaching" in the Epilogue.

Back in the days when I used to worry a lot about what other people thought of me, I would have responded to Dr. Smart's stirring and stimulating address of yesterday with a large load of guilt and anger. That is, after the excitement of the hour had settled down, and I began to see myself a little more clearly. I would have started to feel guilty and angry.

Guilty—because I am all three of the kinds of preachers Dr. Smart told me I shouldn't be. I am the *topical* preacher who is concerned about the issues of the day, about the church's role in them, about myself, and about you. I also think I have some wisdom about these things and would want to share it with you from time to time. And I am an *exegetical* preacher. I get fascinated with biblical texts. I climb into them, scramble over them, get in under them, count the words, puzzle over the syntax—and sometimes get so excited about what I'm finding in the text that I never really come out! And I am also an *expository* preacher. I like to take a text, understand it concretely, and then apply it in my life and in the lives of other people. I don't always wrestle with the problems of the text, but rather find something in the text that I want to preach about. So—if it is a bad thing to be a topical preacher, an exegetical preacher, and an expository preacher—then I am guilty. I am the man. What must I do to be saved? If I can't be a topical preacher or an exegetical preacher or an expository preacher—in the name of God, what can I be?

85

And so there is guilt. And anger.

Anger at all of "them" for what they have done to me. They brought me up under topical preaching, then pushed me into exegesis, and then pulled me toward expository preaching. My anger rises as I think about "those rotten liberals" with their wishy-washy topicality, and "those terrible fundies" with their scriptural dogmatism— all *those* people." I am angry at them. Or am I? Really I'm not angry with them at all, but at him—that Smart guy from Toronto who makes me feel guilty about being the way I am. But he is a nice man, somebody I have respected for a long time. I have been carefully trained not to get angry at nice people, especially when I know that what they say is true and I even agree with them. So, really, I am angry at myself.

In letting myself feel that anger, and guilt, I learn important things about myself: When I am confronted and judged I feel guilty. This puts me in touch with the things I care about. It also makes clear to me what I want to be, and what I don't want to be. My anger empowers me to think thoughts that I would not otherwise allow into consciousness. As I say, all this was back in the days when I used to be moved by anger and guilt—like yesterday! So what shall I do now?

I have a perfectly good sermon left over from the opening convocation which was snowed out last month, and I had promised myself to find an occasion to share these thoughts with you—this must be the occasion. That sermon grew out of Luke 11:9-10, the scripture text which the student body president selected for the convocation. I feel some responsibility to take that text seriously. And I also have some additional texts which are the lectionary readings for today. I have climbed into them, scrambled over them, tried to get under them, have prayed over them, and have some things to say about them. I'll do a little of all three kinds of preaching: topical, exegetical, expository. And I welcome you to participate in the occasion by sharing your reflections on the scriptures as we meditate prayerfully over these texts in this hour of worship.

This means that I have decided to preach, but not to deliver a sermon. Do you get that distinction? While I have prepared myself to share some thoughts with you, I have not prepared a sermon which I now intend to deliver to you. I am going to do that tonight at a church here in Lancaster, and tomorrow I'll be doing the same in a church in Birmingham, Alabama, at a city-wide Lenten service. For those occasions I have to prepare and deliver a sermon. *There* I am a stranger. I have a role to play. I have a task to perform among people with whom I have no opportunity or responsibility to interact. But *here* I don't need to give a performance. Here, in the context of our community, I want to use another mode of preaching which is called a homily. And, as in the manner of the synagogue, I will stand up in a moment to read some scripture and then sit down to comment on it. If you have a word of testimony from these texts, if God is speaking to you through these words, then God has empowered and anointed you to speak a word as well as me. So to the first text. "Ask, and it will be given you; seek, and you will find; knock, and it will be opened to you" (Luke 11:9).

On the surface this sounds like an open invitation to the worst kind of self-seeking—a promise that if we ask, we get. At a deeper level I see it as an invitation to trust and test the grace of God. I also want to suggest that this is an invitation both to test and learn to trust our *wants*. For the basic question raised by the text is: What do I do about what I want?

I was raised in a middle-class family where it wasn't nice to want. And if you wanted, you didn't ask. Even if you were offered something, you declined gracefully by saying "Thank you, but I really don't want that." Yet here is a text that says: "Nice or not, ask for what you want." This text is especially tempting during Lent—a season which traditionally encourages us to practice self-denial, to give things up, and not to ask for what we want because that would be selfish!

In light of this, I think it providential that we have been given I Kings 3:5-13 and Matthew 20:17-28 as readings for this day in Lent.

In the first reading, God comes to Solomon in a dream (how often God came to people in dreams during ancient times) and says: "Ask something of me, and I will give it to you." Isn't that incredible. It reminds me of a phrase in one of the ancient prayers we sometimes use here in chapel: "Oh thou who art more ready to hear than we are to ask . . ." The truth that God wants us to ask is kept alive in our liturgy. Even when we fail to preach that truth, our prayers carry the message. One reason I avoid that prayer is that it is genuinely frightening. The words of the prayer force me to ask myself—what do I really want? And then I wonder—If I could really get what I wanted, what would I ask for? The text has made it clear enough: I can have what I ask for. The only question is: What do I want? If I believe that I am, indeed, going to get what I want, I must be very careful what I ask for. But I can be too careful. Remember the folk tales about the three wishes, and how some people used up their three wishes trying to figure out what the right question was? And just when they figure out the right question, they run out of wishes! So let us be direct. What do I want?

Solomon presents himself in these verses as a young man who wants to "do what is right." He is concerned with appearances and wants to behave in a way that is acceptable. I think we can all understand that. But there are two other things in the lesson that concern me this morning. The first one has become especially meaningful to me. Solomon says, "I serve you in the midst of a people whom you have chosen" (I Kings 3:8 NAB). This helps me understand something that has been happening with me during the seven years I have been at Lancaster Seminary. When I came here to be president in 1970, I had a very strong sense that God had called me, and I had a very clear notion of what I was called here to do. I wasn't really very interested in what anybody else thought about why they were here, or what they thought they were doing. It took me a couple of years to realize that you people had a sense of vocation, too. I came to see that most of you believe God has called you here, that it is your vocation to be in this place. So now I have a text which explains all this to me. "I serve you in the midst of a people whom you have chosen."

Each year when the new students arrive, I am especially sensitive to this question of calling. During orientation it becomes clear to me that there are some members of the incoming class whom I would not have chosen if I had anything to do with it. And at graduation each year there are some who come across the platform to whom I would rather not give a diploma. But that is not the issue because it is not my function to decide who gets in and who gets out. Instead, I am to learn what it means to believe that we are *all* called. Each of us has a special vocation. That's what we have in common. That is the basis of our life together in the seminary and in the church. As we read in John's Gospel, "You have not chosen me but I have chosen you." I realize that I didn't want to believe that about everyone. What has now opened up to me is the awareness that other people have that same desire and that God has answered all our prayers. We can understand ourselves as people chosen by God, called together in his name, gathered for his purposes. Reflecting on this text reminds me that my wants have changed—what I now desire is different from what I wanted before. I am delighted to know that I can change and to know also that I understand these changes in the light of the ancient scripture: I serve in the midst of a people whom God has chosen. And now I know that I want it that way.

But meanwhile, back to Solomon and his wants. What does he want? What did he ask for? He asked for understanding so that he could be a good and wise king. This was, of course, a very selfish thing. He wanted to be a great king. He wanted to be a good king, and so he asked for what he needed to become what he wanted. I am coming to understand that being in touch with my deepest wants makes it clear to me what I need, rather than the other way around. Solomon was straightforward about his wants. He asked for what he wanted, and he got it. Then, in that miracle we find throughout the scriptures, he got not only what he wanted—but more! As Jesus put it, "Seek ye first the

kingdom of God, and everything else will be yours."
And so it is in this text. Solomon gets what he asks
for—and more. "I give you also what you have not
asked, both riches and honor, so that no other king
shall compare with you, all your days" (I Kings 3:13). I
choose to believe that Solomon's selfishness was
transformed because it was set in the context of
service. He wanted to be a great king. There is no doubt
about that. But he wanted to be a great king so he could
serve the Lord.

Selfishness in the context of service is transformed
—but it does not cease to be selfishness. This is what I
have been thinking about recently, and I am coming to
understand that being close to my wants brings me
close to God, and that what God wants most from me is
that I be honest about my wants. I have discovered this
spiritually as well as practically. The more I pay
attention to the language of prayer, the more aware I
am that the language of prayer is the language of
desire. I have also come to discover that the most vital
prayers in my life are those in which I am most direct
about my wants. And in this way I have also come to
understand that I *want* to be a pious person, that I
want to know the reality of prayer, that I *want* to be a
faithful servant of Jesus Christ. I *know* that this is what
I *want*. There is nothing unselfish about it at all.

In Matthew 20:17-28 we have the same kind of
thing. Jesus and his disciples are going up to
Jerusalem. He tells them that it is going to be really
tough now. The end is in sight. Options are closing
down. Ahead lies not simply service, but suffering and
sacrifice. Then this Zebedee woman comes along, the
mother of James and John. She is coming to ask for

something. She has heard the word "ask and it will be given you," and she has believed it. She is coming honestly and straightforwardly to ask for what she wants. Jesus looks at her and asks, "What do you want?" He doesn't say, "What do you think you can get?" or "What do you think it would be nice to ask for?" but "What do you want?" She knows that what she wants is the very best for her boys. She says, in effect, "I hear what you say about the trouble ahead in Jerusalem. I don't know how things are going to go, but however they turn out, I want my sons to be right there with you—one on your right hand and one on your left hand."

Now we can read this text as if it were a pushy mother seeking privilege for her sons. Or we can see her request in terms of Christian commitment. I can identify with her desire to get the very best for her own. That is what I want, too. I want the very best for myself, for my family, for my students, for our seminary, for our church. And there is nothing wrong with this. It is selfish, and self-seeking, but when Jesus puts my wants in the context of suffering and sacrifice, they become transformed.

It may be that the sons of Zebedee were so busy plotting their campaign for status that they didn't hear Jesus' speech on the road about what was going to happen in Jerusalem. I choose to believe that they heard, and that they thought it over. Later on when Jesus asks, "Do you really think you are ready to go through with this?" they say, "Yes, we think we can." And he says: "Do you really know what you are asking? Do you really want to die with me? If you really want to then you are already on the road with me. Stay close to me. I can't guarantee how it will come out for you in the end. But you know what you want. You have been straightforward about it. And that is good."

And then there were the other ten, the passive-aggressive complainers. They wanted the same thing for themselves, but they were "too nice" to ask. Therefore there was only one thing they could do, and that was to blame someone else. There they were, angry and hostile Christians, their self-righteousness and frustration tumbling over their guilt and anger saying in effect, "You shouldn't have asked for that—it's selfish." Which means, "We wish we had the nerve to ask for what we really want!"

Then Jesus talks about how it is to be in the new community of faith. He begins by reminding them of how outsiders act. "Those gentiles, when they get power, they really lord it over each other. They show off. This is not how it is to be among you. You know the way it is when people have titles like Doctor, Professor, Reverend, Director, President, Priest, Father—whatever! People think status symbols make them great. They just don't seem to understand that lording it over each other is not going to get them anywhere." Then Jesus makes it very plain indeed: "If you want to be great, if you want to be first, here is how to do it. Become the servant of all." So the real issue at stake is: What kind of greatness and what kind of excellence? For me, Lent is a time to get in touch with my wants. The question is not what should I want so that I can be regarded as a nice person, but am I ready to make a full commitment to greatness which requires a radical sacrifice.

As I wrestle with this, I find these texts calling me to

a stunning simplicity. God said to Solomon: "Ask for what you want." Jesus said to the mother of James and John, "What do you want?" I ask myself, What do I really want? Deep inside of me I become aware that what I want most is to discover those gifts and graces in my life that will empower me to fulfill my calling. Just as Solomon wanted to be a great king in Israel, so I want to be a great president for this seminary. And as the mother of James and John wanted her sons to be close to Christ, so I want my students, my friends, my colleagues to be close to Christ. I really want this.

When I am honest about this want, I hear the rest that goes with it: I am called to share my dream with others and to accept the common sense of vocation that Solomon expressed so well. "I serve you in the midst of a people whom you have chosen." I hear the call to servanthood and sacrifice. In the days of Lent as we look toward the renewal of our lives at Easter, we know something more of the cost of the cross and what it means to lay down one's life for others. There is pain and suffering, but no confusion. The issue is clear. If I would be great, if you would be great, we will become servants of all. And if this seminary would be first, it must become the servant of God's kingdom. Is that what we really want?

So during Lent consider the questions put to Solomon and to the mother of James and John. It is an appropriate time to test and trust the grace of God. It is a time to hear and believe again. "Ask and it will be given you, seek and you will find, knock and it will be opened. For everyone who asks receives, and everyone who seeks finds." The doors of life will open to those who pray for what they want.

EPILOGUE

Confessions
of a Traveling Preacher

As a traveling preacher I have the opportunity to preach the same sermon to different congregations. On the one hand this means that I have time to practice, to repeat the sermon, to polish and perfect it. On the other hand, I have the opportunity to use the same material with different people. They provide a variety of perspectives on the material that I would not otherwise have, so being a traveling preacher is a great learning opportunity for me.

I have developed a theory that justifies my practice of repeating sermons: I can't travel with new material. I need to be very sure of what I am going to say so I can concentrate my energy on the congregation, and not on the sermon. This means that I do not see preaching primarily as the preparation and delivery of sermons, but rather the structuring of an occasion for Christian communication. What the preacher says, perhaps in the form of a sermon, is simply a catalyst that enables the congregation to have something in common. What they have in common is their commitment to the gospel and their life in the church. The occasion of preaching is an opportunity to get in touch with these realities.

The local pastor never has time to practice. He or she preaches a sermon to the congregation, and that is it

—once and done. But the local pastor has an opportunity after the preaching to see what effects the sermon has in the lives of people, to follow up with individual persons the questions and comments they have about it, and to see it as part of a total ministry. A pastoral relationship is the background to preparing a sermon and that same relationship continues after the preaching. As a traveling preacher I never develop that kind of relationship to a congregation, but I do develop an attachment to my sermons.

On Repeating Sermons

Pastors become terribly concerned that they not repeat themselves, lest they be considered lazy or forgetful. It has been my experience as a pastor and teacher that very few people ever catch anything the first time they hear it. Even in seminary classes where students have their notebooks out and are listening carefully to prepare themselves for a final exam, I have often had to repeat something four and five times, illustrate it several different ways, and then repeat it again in order to make sure that the students both heard and understood it. Therefore, the pastor who fears repetition just doesn't understand one of the very important dynamics of communication. It is "precept upon precept, line upon line" that finally communicates.

It seems to me that repetition has been good both for the congregation and for me. For me it has meant wrestling with the same theme over and over and over again, turning it this way and that to see new facets and dimensions of it. And sometimes I have become aware that I must keep preaching a sermon over and over again until it becomes clear and convincing to me! For instance, the sermon on prayer which I have included here, kept reminding me of my desire to learn to pray, until I finally got around to it—years later.

The People's Part in Preaching

I have become convinced that the congregation brings at least as much to the preaching situation as the preacher does. Just in terms of time and animal energy, the congregation puts more into the preaching than the pastor does. Even if the pastor has spent twenty or thirty hours that week preparing the sermon, a congregation of a hundred or more sitting there and listening to the sermon for fifteen to thirty minutes are spending more person hours listening to the sermon than the pastor spent preparing it. Of course, different forms of labor are involved, but I hope the point is clear.

At a deeper level, members of the congregation bring not only their time and their attention, but their whole lives to the situation. It is unlikely that the pastor is ever dealing with a theme that is totally foreign to people in the congregation. They have heard sermons on that general subject before (they may even have heard sermons on that particular text) and have given some thought to the particular question or concern being dealt with in the sermon. Therefore, it seems important to me that the pastor take into account the very important contribution that the congregation is making to his or her preaching—not simply by listening but

97

by bringing to the preaching situation their own prayerful understandings, personal experiences, and Christian commitments.

So when I travel around, I am not interested in coming up with new material that will impress the congregation. Rather, I come into the situation with some ideas and words (that sound like a "sermon" to the congregation) to provide a clear and simple focus for my thoughts and feelings. As I take my place behind the pulpit and begin to speak, I feel that I want to give my full attention and energy, not to what I am saying, but to what is happening in the congregation. Being "sure of my material" I am free to look at their faces and not at my notes. I am free to open myself to the congregation, seeking their response and responding to them. Sometimes the response comes in the form of laughter to a comment I have made. Sometimes it comes in the form of an almost tangible silence as we enter together into the consideration of the text or a theme that touches us deeply. At other times the congregation reacts with confusion or hostility. In each instance, I want to be able to sense their reactions and respond appropriately to them. In my own case, I find I must be sure of my material before I am free to change it, to improvise, to cut it short, to expand on it.

It is a little like walking. I have to put one foot down firmly and find a place where I can be steady before I can move the other one ahead. I grope around for a place where I can put one foot down, and when that one is firmly placed I lift the other and move it forward. In the preaching situation I also need to be sure of one thing at a time, providing a basis for moving ahead.

When I am in a familiar setting, such as the seminary

chapel, I feel free to experiment with new material. This was also true when I served as interim pastor in a congregation for a period of time. But in a new situation I always begin with my old sermons. Within a month or two I am familiar enough with the local situation to begin experimenting with new material. But when I am on the road, entering one strange situation after another, I always travel with familiar material.

On Finishing Sermons

Another thing I'm learning. No matter how long I preach, I never seem to finish. I now have a different notion about "finishing things." It doesn't really bother me now if I don't "get it done." As a teacher and preacher I used to try to "get it in," "make it fit," "cover the subject." But now I think preaching ought to be more like a slice of life than like a work of art. Students in the seminary have reminded me of this. Sometimes when I've encouraged one of them to dig deeper into Old Testament or church history he or she will say, "Oh, I had that." Isn't that sad. To feel like you've finished something, when you've only begun.

As a traveling preacher I am frustrated by churches that have two services on Sunday morning, usually at 9:30 and 11:00 a.m. By the time I've finished preaching at the 9:30 service I'm through for the day. I often wish they would tape the sermon and play it back to the eleven o'clock crowd. But no! I have to crank up and start all over again. Still, one advantage of two services is that if I don't finish the sermon at the first service,

I can finish it at the second! One time I began preaching at the eleven o'clock service with: "And now, as I was saying at 9:30." I simply picked up where I had left off and went on preaching. As I recall I didn't even "finish" at the second service. Over coffee after the service the discussion went on for half an hour more! Perhaps I, as a visiting preacher, should work harder to finish my sermon. But the local pastor shouldn't worry about that because he or she has a built-in opportunity to keep the dialogue going—over coffee, in homes, etc.—whereas I miss the chance to continue the dialogue. If I were a local pastor again I don't think I'd ever try to "finish." As the student said of his studies in Bible and theology: "I've had that," so a parishioner could say of a sermon on love or fear or grace: "We've heard that." But isn't that sad. If Schubert could write an Unfinished Symphony, any pastor can preach an Unfinished Sermon once in a while. (I'm not finished with this idea, but I'll stop here!)

There is one potentially negative aspect of this practice of preaching the same sermon over and over. I worry from time to time about the possibility of a kind of mental laziness setting in. If I go around "doing my thing" and repeating a lot of old material, perhaps I am cutting myself off from the stimulus of new thoughts. But I find that sermons have a life of their own—some of them grow and some of them die. Some of my sermons do not give themselves to repetition. I preach them once or twice, but tend not to use them again. Others I use dozens—even hundreds—of times. From this I have learned that some themes are perhaps more central to the Christian faith than others, that some of the clues I have followed are more productive than others, and that some sermons are more like good seeds that, when placed in a variety of settings, continue to sprout and grow. It is sermons of this sort that I have gathered together in this little volume to share with friends. I send them forth in the hope that they will be of use in the church and that I will get some feedback from people who read them. I hope those who have already heard them will see how much they have contributed to them.

About Introductions

When I first saw these sermons typed out I realized that most of them don't have proper introductions. They just start. This struck me as strange, because when I preach I usually spend a lot of time getting started. In thinking this over, I realized that when I preach I do not introduce a sermon—I introduce myself. This is another way in which I distinguish between preaching to people and delivering a sermon.

Sermons require an introduction to the sermon. *Preaching* requires introducing the preacher. And that's what I do. I may spend up to ten minutes just introducing myself, reading the scriptures, and getting started. Usually I take three to five minutes. I have a theory that there's no point talking to people unless they are listening, and when I preach I assume there are two things I have to overcome before the congregation will listen. First, most of them believe I have three strikes against me. Therefore, I must first assure them that they are going to understand what I have to say. More than that I want to let them know that I need their help to get the preaching done because if the congregation feels that they can merely sit and receive, they don't get involved. That is why I actually enlist their support. Second, many people get used to hearing their own pastor. They know what he or she believes and what he or she is going to say. In most congregations the preaching is good, people are used to listening, and they are waiting to hear what I have to say. But some congregations have a smaller attendance when a traveling preacher shows up—even a seminary president! They have come to believe and trust their pastor. They look forward to his or her messages. And they don't know why they should turn out for a stranger. I don't want to be a stranger either, so under normal circumstances (which means most of the time) I begin by using the following form of introduction. I think I used it for the first time at Trinity United Church of Christ in York, Pennsylvania, in 1975. It worked so well, I have used it regularly ever since. (If you are troubled by the lack of introductions to the sermons in this book, just flip back here and read my all-purpose introduction, then go back to where the preaching starts.)

An All-Purpose Introduction to the Sermons in This Book

In a rather formal, almost oratorical, tone of voice, I say:

"It is a privilege, and a pleasure . . . and something of
a problem to be your preacher this morning."

Usually the word "problem" gets an immediate
response: amusement, surprise, sympathy, curiosity.
Then, I say a few things about "privilege" because I am
often invited to preach at the dedication of a building, or
the anniversary of a congregation. Recently I was
invited for a 250th anniversary! It *is* a privilege and an
honor to be included in such occasions, and so I enjoy
sharing this. It also gives me an opportunity to
recognize some contribution the congregation and/or
pastor has made, and to bring in the greetings of the
seminary. So much for privilege.

My "pleasure" is expressed for the invitation, not
only to be present and represent the seminary, but for
the opportunity to preach. I usually say:

"As a preacher without a pulpit of his own I depend
entirely on invitations of this sort to have a chance to
preach at all. It is always a pleasure to worship God
and preach the gospel. And it is a pleasure to be here
as your preacher this morning. But it is also
something of a problem."

I look again for that response—which by now is usually
curiosity—and I try to satisfy that curiosity by
commenting on five things: the pulpit, the acoustics,
the choir, the clock, and the subject of the sermon.
Here is a sample:

"Now it isn't a *big* problem, so don't worry. As a
traveling preacher it takes me a few minutes to get
settled into a strange place and to feel at home. You
have received me warmly, and I appreciate the
generous introduction. The problems are much
more practical.

103

"Like this pulpit. You know, every pulpit is a little different. There are basically two kinds, the kind you stand behind and the kind you walk into. I see the backside of lots of pulpits. In fact I seldom see that frontside you are looking at right now. Have you ever seen the inside/backside of this one? It's really very neat/messy. There's a special kind of junk that collects in pulpits, you know."

(In the pulpit of the First Presbyterian Church of Kalamazoo there is a huge red fire extinguisher. And in the Presbyterian Church in Towson, Maryland, there is a telephone! Almost every pulpit has something unusual on which I can comment.)

"And the acoustics. I have a theory that there's no point talking to people unless they are listening. And they can't listen unless they can hear. Can you hear me if I talk like this?

(This usually gets some more response from people and lets them know I want to be heard.)

"And the choir. As a traveling preacher I never know where to find the choir. Sometimes they are in a balcony in the back. That way I can see them. Sometimes they are on either side. And sometimes they are behind me. I see your choir is _____. I'll want to turn around every once in a while to look at them—to keep my eye on them and keep them awake.

(Actually, the choir is flattered to be included, and is usually grateful for the reference.)

"Now about clocks. I have a theory that the clocks in churches are put where they are needed most. If the congregation needed them most, they'd be up front where you could see them. But usually they are in the back—for the preacher. I'm glad you have a big clock back there, because I have a tendency to get carried away and preach for a long time. Actually, since I don't get a chance to preach regularly, I suffer from a kind of homiletical build-up and have more need to preach than you have to listen. So I need to watch the clock. Recently I was preaching in a church where the service began at eleven o'clock. I asked the pastor how long I should preach. He said: 'You can preach as long as you want, but the people go home at noon!' I can see by the clock that if I'm going to preach, I had better get started.

(At this point the congregation is usually ready to settle down for the sermon—and may even be getting impatient!)

"Finally there is the problem of what to preach. This is always a problem for a traveling preacher. I'm a stranger. I don't know who you are or what you are doing here. You can't expect from me the kind of preaching you get from your pastor. He/she knows you. You share a life together in the congregation and this community. He/she can preach to you out of that common life. I can't do that. I must find something else as a basis for preaching. So this morning I've chosen to . . . ."

At this point I make reference to the specific occasion (anniversary, dedicaton, etc.), to a season of the church year (Lent, Advent, Pentecost, etc.), to some current issue in the denomination or the region, or I simply say:

"Since I don't know what is of interest and importance to you, I decided to share something that is of interest and importance to me. It is based on the scripture lessons for today and is an attempt to share with you something out of my faith and experience which I hope will speak to your faith and experience. In so far as you know what I am talking about, and find it meaningful, we will experience the mystery of our unity in the Body of Christ. So let us pray." After a brief prayer I either read the lessons or just start preaching!

You see, this is not so much an introduction to a sermon about *to be delivered* as an introduction to preaching about *to happen.* It is really an introduction to myself, in the context of which I have a chance to test the reactions of the congregation, offer them a chance to see me deal with my initial nervousness, and enlist them in the act of preaching which is about to happen.

Preaching as Performance

Reactions to preaching are not always illuminating or instructive. Some people thank me for my "lectures," but I do not think I am lecturing. Other people thank me for my "lessons," and I have no idea that I am teaching. Sometimes they say: "Enjoyed it." And who knows what that means? But whatever I've been doing, I am aware that preaching always looks a little like a performance because in a place of worship there are all the signs of a performance: the stage, the audience, the lights. With all of that, it's very hard to resist the temptation to perform.

Søren Kierkegaard used this image to point out that places of worship always look very much like theaters and that therefore congregations very easily get the idea that they are supposed to act like an audience. Like an audience they observe what goes on up front (the preaching and the music) and then decide whether they like it or not. And like a critical audience they judge this performance in relation to others. But, suggests Kierkegaard, when we understand what is going on, when we really preach and when we really worship, we know that there is a difference. True, there is a stage and an audience. The difference is that we are all on stage, and God is the audience. We are all in church to perform. But what is the purpose of the preacher? The preacher is like a prompter in the wings, giving us a text by which to examine our lives in the presence of God.

This is really what I'm trying to do. I am a performer. I stand up there in the pulpit and perform. There's no doubt about that, and I enjoy the response to my performance. I wouldn't have it otherwise. But what I intend in my preaching is that we shall be jointly engaged together in an act of reflection and of devotion, in an act of searching and learning. Although I do not stand in the wings, I am a prompter with a text. Preaching is presenting a text.

Phillips Brooks said that preaching is communicating the truth through personality. I think that's true. Therefore, the focus of preaching is personal—the preacher, the congregation, and the Person of Christ. Focusing on the *sermon* can get in the way, especially if the sermon is too well prepared. A well-prepared sermon comes at me like a stainless steel ball—heavy and smooth with no rough edges, nothing hanging out to hook me. On the other hand, the risk is that *preaching* might focus too much on the preacher—her or his personality. Yet the mystery of the incarnation calls me to just such a risk. Truth through personality

107

—that's the same image of God coming to us in Jesus as the Christ. The Son of Man "hooks" us and holds us. He doesn't "give us something to take home with us." When he fed the multitude there wasn't enough for the week—just enough to get home. A sermon ought not to satisfy—but stir the hunger and whet the appetite—at least that, and maybe more. There is risk in being too personal. But it is a risk I choose to run.

Preaching as Liturgy and Ritual

I also believe that preaching is a liturgical act, almost a ritual act. This does not imply that it is any less dynamic or personal or creative or demanding. It just means that preaching is a formal occasion in which some work (liturgy) is done by people who have a formal (ritual) relationship to each other and to the occasion. Nothing is more ritualized than the "three-point sermon." I paid my respects to that in the first sermon. There are other forms of preaching which make no effort to have "points" at all. And even if there is a logical progression or linear sequence, the formal structure is not emphasized.

We use a variety of modes in the formal structure of a sermon, partly because the whole situation is so ritualized. We are in a specific place (church building, even a special place within the building), at a special time (times vary, but Sunday morning is still prime time), in special positions (in pews, pulpits, choir lofts), doing special things (singing hymns, reading responses, taking up collections, reading the scriptures, and, of course, preaching), playing special roles (preacher, choir, ushers, organist, readers, etc.). Even in those "creative contemporary services," most of these traditional elements are present.

So in being aware of preaching as a liturgical act, I take time to affirm myself as a person in a special place with a special role to play. I also affirm the congregation. They are the people who populate the place, who will be there after I have gone, and who are the most important persons in the preaching which is about to take place. If my kind of preaching is done well, what is said as a sermon is never so important as the relationship between the person who is speaking and the persons who are listening. All are in on the preaching. And, as Kierkegaard said so well—we are not doing this for ourselves, but for the One who calls us into the church to preach and hear the Word.

Whatever Happened to Great Preaching?

I have heard the lament about the decline of preaching in America. Certainly, twenty years ago there were some outstanding preachers who were setting high standards for American pulpits. But there were only a few of them (Buttrick, Sockman, and Fosdick on Manhattan, a few in Chicago and California, and in the major cities of the South.) That wasn't a whole lot of "great preaching." But now, even though there appear to be no "giants" either in print or on the radio, I believe that the average pastor in a Protestant pulpit today is a much better preacher than the majority were in the last generation. He or she is better trained theologically and homiletically and has more access to printed material and electronic equipment, etc. Congregations are more demanding. So to me the theological content and the professional competence of preaching seems to be at an all time high.

But what I do miss is local color. Most of the sermons I hear could be preached anywhere. What the parish pastor can do (and what traveling preachers like myself cannot do) is speak a word of God for a particular people in a particular time and place. There is a sense in which a truly prophetic sermon (that is, one preached in the particularity of a parish) might not make any sense at all to a casual visitor. Now, I know, that is overstating the case, but something like that is true.

Prophetic Preaching in the Parish

Prophetic preaching in the parish is not haranguing the locals about "world issues." It is proclaiming the gospel for a particular time and place. It is not puzzling out and predicting the future. It is calling people to faithfulness here and now.

One of the frustrations of a traveling preacher is his or her inability to do that. The local pastor can. But sometimes a local pastor says to me: "You give them the prophetic word, I can't do it; if I told them the truth, they'd run me out of town." That's a measure of the seriousness of prophetic preaching in the parish; that it can get the local pastor in trouble. As a visitor, I can say anything I want—and the locals can pass it off because *I'm* just passing through. The parish pastor has to be dealt with. He or she cannot be passed off. And he or she *can* get in trouble, because the local pastor can really "tell it like it is," can preach the true and lively word. I pray for a recovery of that kind of prophetic pastoral preaching.

The Best of My Barrel

Preachers often refer to their "sermon barrel." I've never seen a barrel full of sermons, nor met a pastor who kept his or her sermons in one. I assume that the term comes from a time when pastors moved their valuables in barrels, and that one of the most valuable barrels on the moving van was the barrel containing sermons and pastoral records. (If anyone out there knows the derivation of the term, I'd be delighted to hear from you.)

My "barrel" is actually a small set of file folders in which I keep the outlines and notes from the sermons I preach. As a traveling preacher, I also carefully note the dates and places on which I have preached each sermon. I used to do this to make sure I would not repeat myself, feeling that to do so would be an embarrassment both to the congregation and to me. I now do this as a personal record and don't worry about repeating myself. I have already said something about repeating. Here is another confession on the same subject.

I am actually invited to repeat particular sermons. For several years this has been true of the "snake-handling" sermon. More recently, I have had requests for the sermons on prayer and selfishness. I am pleased to accept these invitations; I announce to the congregation that I will be sharing with them some thoughts on which I am still working and ask for their comments and suggestions. I find the response most encouraging. Lay people seem eager to help me preach better sermons. I wish more pastors would engage lay people in this kind of exercise. It might help us toward better preaching in all our pulpits.

I didn't plan to put all this down when I set myself the task of putting together a book of sermons. But in working my sermons over—in trying to translate speech into print which could be read—I discovered that I had developed some ideas about preaching based on the special kind of preaching I have been doing for twenty-five years. So I have shared the best in my barrel—and these Confessions of a Traveling Preacher.